Budget Practices and State Expenditures: Lessons for California

• • •

Jaime Calleja Alderete

2007

Library of Congress Cataloging-in-Publication Data
Alderete, Jaime Calleja, 1975–
Budget practices and state expenditures: lessons for California / Jaime Calleja Alderete.
p. cm.
Includes bibliographical references.
ISBN 978-58213-125-2
1. Budget—California. 2. Fiscal policy—California. I. Title.
HJ2053.C2A43 2007
352.4'809794—dc22
2007003183

PPIC does not take or support positions on any ballot measure or on any local, state, or federal legislation, nor does it endorse, support, or oppose any political parties or candidates for public office.

Research publications reflect the views of the authors and do not necessarily reflect the views of the staff, officers, or Board of Directors of the Public Policy Institute of California.

Foreword

Budget Practices and State Expenditures: Lessons for California is a welcome addition to the literature analyzing state-level public spending. The author, research fellow Jaime Calleja Alderete, takes a careful look at numerous suggestions for improved budget practices to see if they have actually performed as advertised. He reviews practices in all 50 states, focusing on a small number of high-population states that have adopted one or more of six progressive budget practices: funding targets, legislative access, performance measurement, performance management, performance budgeting, and mid-session revision. Florida, Illinois, New York, and Texas have adopted four or more of these practices, and California has adopted only one—mid-session revision. This is popularly known in California as the May revision of the governor's budget.

Numerous commissions, study groups, and academic reports have recommended that California adopt various kinds of improvements to the budget process—especially to bring the state budget into balance and to improve the transparency of the budget to citizens and bond investors alike. Most recently, Governor Arnold Schwarzenegger launched the California Performance Review, which made numerous recommendations for improved budget practices. The vast majority of the review's proposals were abandoned, in part because of a lack of evidence substantiating their claims.

Calleja Alderete's findings are not encouraging when success is measured by the amount of money saved. Only three of the six budget practices saved any money at all, and for them the savings were an average of only 2.1 percent per capita. In some cases the budget practices actually increased the amount of spending in certain areas of spending—for example, government administration and social services. The one budget practice that California uses regularly, mid-session revision, showed some reduction in spending across all the states adopting it—but the average 1.8 percent reduction in per capita spending was not statistically significant. Performance measurement and performance management, as budget practices, had no significant effects on total spending.

These findings, combined with earlier scholarly research that finds little effect of stringent budget rules on total spending across all states, give one pause about the prospects for containing the fundamentally political quality of the budget process—whether at the state, local, or federal level. In California, the state budget is the responsibility of the executive branch, and there is little incentive for any governor to relinquish control over this process. This and other research implies that the myriad special interests embedded in the budget cycle will not easily yield to either simple budget rules or more subtle progressive budget practices. Perhaps that is why Californians—aware of this reality—have had a long history of electing fiscally conservative governors while electing local representatives who are more fiscally liberal. In any event, Calleja Alderete's findings strongly suggest that we should not look elsewhere for solutions to our own budget process—other high-population states are also having a difficult time securing the savings typically advertised by advocates of the most innovative budget practices.

David W. Lyon
President and CEO
Public Policy Institute of California

Summary

California's most recent major fiscal meltdown at the beginning of this decade—featuring unusually large gaps between revenues and expenditures—triggered many policy discussions and measures focused on how to address the state's budget problems. Among the options presented to tackle these issues was reform of the budget process itself. It was not the first time that policymakers had debated budget reform as a way to cope with or prevent fiscal crises; the California Research Bureau reports that in the last 15 years, 18 commissions or study groups have made more than 100 proposals to reform one or several features of the state's budget process (Wear Simmons, 2002). Several recommendations have been proposed repeatedly during different episodes of dire fiscal circumstances. The focus of many of these budget reform studies and recommendations has been on budget rules such as debt limits, or balanced budget requirements, and on understanding how such rules affect spending. However, a good proportion of the budget reform proposals have aimed at less-scrutinized components of the process: budget practices.

Budget practices are the procedural steps and administrative tools used to develop a government's annual budget. Examples include providing specific instructions for agencies' budget requests; defining baselines on which such requests are based; requiring that particular accounting methods are followed; and providing specific information to justify funding decisions, methods, types, and frequency of revenue and caseload forecasts. Budget practices have a wide set of objectives—including increased transparency and timeliness of the budget process, improved accuracy of revenue forecasts, and better management or improved rationality in fund allocation. Although some budget practices might be prescribed by statute, they tend to be discretionary and adapted from year to year as circumstances require.

Budget practices are numerous and diverse and not all of them are likely to affect the outcomes of the budget process in the same manner. Some can influence monetary outcomes such as revenues or expenditures; others can change nonmonetary outcomes such as transparency and accountability. Furthermore, some budget practices may have implications for several of these outcomes, whereas others might have implications for only one. Thus, a thorough understanding of all budget practices requires addressing each of these potential outcomes separately. This report provides a much-needed first effort to understand the effects of budget practices on state expenditures.

The relevance of budget practices for government expenditures rests on the premise that the way the budget is constructed can promote government efficiency, reduce waste, and enhance the rationality of resource allocation. In turn, these effects could lead to savings in government operations, yielding leaner budgets. These prospects, together with recurrent calls for changes in the budget process as a whole, have increased the attractiveness, and heightened the expectations, of budget practice reform.

The key characteristic that links budget practices with spending is their ability to influence the information with which participants in the budget process make their decisions. Three factors make a budget practice more likely to affect spending: It communicates directly the administration's specific financial and policy guidelines; it determines the information available to budget participants at each stage of the process; or it generates information that shapes or justifies funding allocations. By applying these criteria to a series of practices defined by the National Association of State Budget Officers and the National Council of State Legislatures, this report identifies the following six practices by their potential to affect government spending and examines their effect on state expenditures and on spending across budget categories.

1. **Funding targets:** This practice requires that government agencies abide by specific numeric limits to their budget requests. The executive branch communicates these financial objectives through the budget office at the beginning of each budgeting cycle.
2. **Legislative access:** In this practice, the legislature can review budget requests from all agencies when the executive budget office is assembling the proposed budget, that is, before the legislature officially receives the proposed budget from the executive branch. Providing such access changes the information available to legislators when they are considering the allocation of funds. It also provides them with a

better understanding of agencies' and programs' funding needs and potential tradeoffs across programs and government areas as well as with additional time to analyze particular requests and to consider their appropriate funding levels.

3. **Performance measurement:** Government agencies prepare their budget requests with the aid of different types of information, most commonly caseload assumptions and procurement price limits, which are often set by the executive budget office. However, agencies can also rely on performance measures, which indicate their programs' expected outcomes and outputs, usually relative to prespecified objectives. Specific measures differ by type of agency and program but examples include test scores for education agencies, recidivism rates for corrections agencies, and disease prevention rates for health services agencies.
4. **Performance management:** The information on program effectiveness contained in performance measures provides government agencies with a tool to manage their resources and establish priorities more effectively. Performance management informs and shapes agencies' budget requests.
5. **Performance budgeting:** This practice is followed when performance measures provide explicit additional justification for the budget office to decide on proposed funding or for the legislature to approve such requests. Performance budgeting provides additional rationality for spending allocations. For instance, a documented increase in test scores could lead to increases in education expenditures, and evidence of higher recidivism rates could increase resources to corrections agencies.
6. **Mid-session revision:** The forecasts of revenues and caseloads are universally incorporated into the budget proposal submitted to the legislature. Some states update these forecasts while the legislature discusses the budget. These mid-session revisions contribute to the adoption of realistic budgets by incorporating the latest available information on economic conditions that affect revenue and expenditure estimates.

These six budget practices are widespread across the country, but their adoption patterns have changed somewhat among states (Table S.1). From 1988 to 2002, the practices related to performance (measurement, management, and budgeting) experienced the largest growth in adoption in the 50 states. The use of funding targets also experienced some growth. The use of legislative access and mid-session revisions declined during this period.

California's history of budget practices has been less dynamic than in the rest of the country. Mid-session revisions (known more commonly as the May revision) have been a part of the state's budget process for many years, but legislative access has been absent as a practice from California's budget process in modern history. Funding targets were used for several years throughout the 1990s and during the first years of this decade but have not been established as a permanent policy. Finally, the Wilson administration established a performance budgeting pilot program of limited scope (it included only four small agencies) in the mid-1990s but eliminated it four years later.

California's budget practices are also markedly different from those followed by four states that share some important economic, demographic, or historic features with California (Table S.2): Florida, Illinois, New York, and Texas.

This report compares both total and categorical government expenditures in states with and without these budget practices from 1988

Table S.1

The Number of States Following Each Budget Practice, 1988 and 2002

	1988	2002
Funding targets	22	34
Legislative access to requests	42	30
Performance measurement	8	38
Performance management[a]	8	19
Performance budgeting	8	19
Mid-session revisions	19	14

[a]The data for 2002 correspond to the data for 2000, the last available year for this practice.

Table S.2

Budget Practices in Selected States, 2005

	California	Florida	Illinois	New York	Texas
Funding targets			X	X	
Legislative access		X			X
Performance measurement		X	X	X	X
Performance management		X	X	X	X
Performance budgeting		X	X	X	X
Mid-session revision	X	X	X		X

SOURCE: Direct contact with states' budget offices and legislatures' websites.

to 2002. It finds that after controlling for all the major determinants of expenditures, only three of the six budget practices affect government spending in a significant way (Table S.3). More specifically, states that followed funding targets spent 1.7 percent less than states without it. Moreover, these effects are not immediate, taking up to three years and sometimes more than 15 years to have a significant effect. States that used legislative access spent 2 percent less than states that did not. This relationship is steady from the second to the ninth year following the introduction of this practice, and its significance fades gradually through

Table S.3

Summary of the Effects of Budget Practices on State Expenditures

	Effect on Total Spending (%)	Categories with Similar Qualitative Effects
Funding targets	–1.7	Public safety, environment, K–12 education, higher education, transportation
Legislative access	–2.1	Government administration, environment and housing, higher education, social services, transportation
Performance measurement	Not significant	—
Performance management	Not significant	—
Performance budgeting	–2.0	K–12 education
Mid-session revision	Not significant	—

time. Performance budgeting reduced the size of the budget by 2 percent on average. The associated reductions in expenditures take place right after the adoption of this practice but are also significant in longer time horizons.

Neither performance measurement nor performance management was significantly linked to government expenditures. Similarly, even though states with mid-session revisions spent 1.8 percent less on average than states without this practice, its effects on spending were not statistically significant.

Similar to their effects on total expenditures, funding targets reduce spending in all areas with the exception of government administration, higher education, health, and social services. Legislative access reduces spending mostly on government administration, environment and housing, higher education, social services, and transportation but increases health expenditures by 3 percent. Performance budgeting also affects the composition of the budget, reducing spending on K–12 and higher education and increasing environment, housing, and transportation expenditures.

The report's findings provide guidelines to policymakers interested in budget process reform in California. First, although the state can implement funding targets on an as-needed basis, the report's findings suggest that adopting this practice permanently could contribute to leaner budgets in the long run. Second, the evidence suggests that implementing performance budgeting has led to long-run lower spending levels. Third, the main economic cost of implementing this practice—developing performance measures—has not been high or significant enough to outweigh the spending reductions derived from performance budgeting. Finally, California could enable legislative access to budget requests simultaneous with the preparation of the executive budget, although doing so might alter the balance of budgetary power between the executive and legislative branches. For this reason, adopting legislative access most likely becomes a political issue rather than an economic one and deserves further careful evaluation.

This report's examination of the relationship between budget practices and expenditures is only a first step in a study of the consequences of budget practice reform as a whole but a valuable one. First, although budget practices have several potential implications beyond expenditure levels, government expenditures are informative because of their accessibility and ease of understanding. Second, because calls for budget practice reform arise over and over again when state budgets are particularly tight, this study helps set down definitely just how much money can realistically be saved by implementing some budget practices. By establishing what budget practices can and cannot do for spending, this research enables the policy debate to move beyond it and to focus on other aspects of budgeting, such as revenues, transparency, accountability, and creditors' perceptions of state management practices. In addition, these results can provide an objective basis for discussions of the more indirect implications of budget practices, including the consequences of change on the political and budgetary power balance between the executive and legislative branches of government, or comparison of the factors that make the adoption of some practices more likely in some states than in others. All these questions pose substantial conceptual and methodological challenges worth future research efforts.

Contents

Figures

Tables

Acknowledgments

This report incorporates contributions from several individuals. I am especially grateful to those who devoted their valuable time to review this document, including Diane Cummins of the Office of the President pro tem of the California State Senate; Tracy Gordon of PPIC; David Neumark of PPIC and the Economics Department of the University of California, Irvine; Hillary Hoynes of the Economics Department of the University of California, Davis; Daniel Mitchell of the UCLA School of Management; and Fred Silva of the New California Network. No less useful was the early feedback of my colleagues Marianne Bitler of PPIC, Kim Rueben of the Tax Policy Center and the Urban Institute, and Jon Sonstelie of the Economics Department of the University of California, Santa Barbara. Mark Baldassare and Max Neiman of PPIC and Paul Lewis of Arizona State University offered constant guidance and encouragement throughout all stages of this project. The clarity of the report was greatly improved by the efforts of Richard Greene. Last, but definitely not least, Kate Jordan's contributions were crucial for the completion of this report. Although the input of all these people improved the quality of this report tremendously, I am solely responsible for all the report's findings, conclusions, omissions, or errors.

1. Introduction

For several years, a considerable amount of effort and brainpower has been devoted to formulating recommendations to modify California's budget process. According to the California Research Bureau, in the last 15 years, 18 commissions, study groups, or academic studies have made about 110 recommendations or proposals to address various problems in the state's budget process—including the budget document's lack of clarity, the insufficient degree of accountability of government agencies to the legislature, recurrent unbalanced budgets, outdated administration of government programs, and more (Wear Simmons, 2002). Although the characteristics of these problems differ and therefore inspire different solutions, a majority of recommendations focus on changes to two sets of policies: budget rules and budget practices.

Budget practices are the sequential steps and administrative tools and methods used in the development of the state's budget. They are mostly aimed at enhancing management, increasing the efficiency of government operations, and providing better information to support budget decisions. Budget practices do not establish restrictions on the final size of the budget (like monetary limits or increases relative to economic indicators do), are not procedural (like vote requirements or frequency of budgeting are), and may or may not be engraved in statute or law. As a consequence, their use throughout the budget process can be discretionary. Budget practices are used by individual government agencies as well as by the entire executive and legislative branches. Examples of such practices include instructions and requirements for creating budget requests, deadlines for their submission, and the timing and nature of agency hearings before the legislature. Budget practices shape how the budget is made.

Budget rules, by contrast, are aimed at shaping what the budget should look like. They are restrictions or requirements established by law and are explicitly aimed at controlling budgetary outcomes such as revenues, expenditures, or debt. California's appropriations limit (Proposition 4), minimum guarantee for education spending (Proposition 98), and its recently approved debt limit (Proposition 58) are examples of these rules.

The claims that California's budget practices are in need of serious reform accelerated as a consequence of the economic downturn in the state at the beginning of the decade. Some concerns were raised at the beginning of the Schwarzenegger administration in 2004, with the release of the California Performance Review. The commission's report on the state budget process described it as "broken" and lacking information to link resources to actual government services (California Performance Review, 2004). This was not an isolated perception. In its 2005 national evaluation of state government performance, *Governing* magazine assigned its worst grade to California (Barrett et al., 2005). Similarly, the California Budget Project stated that the state's budget practices adversely affect the budget process's openness and transparency, identified weaknesses in the way the state updates its revenue estimates, and pointed out its lack of contextual information to frame budgetary decisions (California Budget Project, 2006).

Despite the importance of understanding budget practices, our knowledge of budget process reform is heavily skewed toward the relationship between budget rules and government expenditures. A well-established body of research examines experiences across states that have different budget rules to gauge their effects on spending. The driving principle behind these studies is that fiscal constitutions, defined by different configurations of budget rules, should limit the policy choices available to the government (Brennan and Buchanan, 1980).

Extensive reviews of this literature show that budget rules do not always constrain expenditures successfully (Besley and Case, 2003). For example, even tax and expenditure limits expected to be binding have no effect on expenditure levels (Rueben, 1997; Shadbegian, 1996)—although no-deficit carryover rules and tax and expenditure limits reduce governments' ability to promptly adjust taxes and expenditures when they are confronted with unexpected economic shocks (Poterba, 1994a). Supermajority requirements for tax increases reduce taxes as a proportion of income (Knight, 2000). Anti-deficit rules affect the relationship between the cost of borrowing and the time to maturity of government debt (Poterba, 1994b) as well as its interest rate (Goldstein and Woglom, 1992) and the spread on bond yields (Poterba and Rueben, 1999). Finally, a governor's ability to veto specific items in the budget contributes to reductions in expenditures but only when the executive and legislative branches are controlled by opposing political parties (Holtz-Eakin, 1988). In sum, although budget rules do matter in some cases, the empirical evidence is inconclusive on whether anti-deficit rules universally reduce expenditures or taxes (Poterba, 1997).

There has been less exploration of the effects of implementing different budget practices and, in particular, on their relationship with government expenditures. Some studies show that states using previous expenditures as budget baselines spend more than those where the baseline is pegged to current levels of service, although the growth rate of expenditures is higher in the latter group (Crain and Crain, 1998). Others use several budget practices and rules to construct an index of budget transparency and conclude that state expenditures increase with transparency (Alt, Dreyer-Lassen, and Skilling, 2001). One explanation for this finding is that when voters know the workings of the budget better, they are willing to support a larger government (Ferejohn, 1999). Finally, there is some evidence that states that use information on the outcomes and outputs of their programs to make budgeting decisions spend less than states where no such information is used in the budget process (Crain and O'Roark, 2004).

The relative sparseness of research on the effects of budget practices is partially a consequence of the inherent difficulty in quantifying the government outcomes associated with them. These difficulties include accuracy in assessing program needs, timeliness of budgeting decisions, and judgment of the quality of government services, among others. However, some of those outcomes could have measurable consequences, at least indirectly. In particular, it is commonly claimed that improving the way the budget is constructed as well as the information on which it is based leads to increased government efficiency, which in turn affects government spending (National Conference of State Legislatures, 2004; California Performance Review, 2004).

Furthermore, the recurrent calls for reform especially during fiscal downturns indicate high expectations about the ability of budget practices to control government expenditures. It is then crucial to evaluate these claims: Policymakers and taxpayers need to know first if budget practice reform can reduce spending to next evaluate whether those reductions (if any) translate into more efficient government. And if there is empirical evidence supporting a relationship between budget practices and expenditures—which might not necessarily be negative—the magnitude of such effects becomes important. Even learning that improved budget practices are inconsequential to government spending is a valuable lesson because attention can then be focused on other potential positive outcomes such as improved transparency and accountability. These outcomes might not be easily measurable, but they provide relevant criteria on which to evaluate the state's budget process.

This report's targeted focus on government expenditures comes at the cost of not uncovering links between all budget practices and all their potential implications. Although this scope is very specific, it is only the first in a series of steps toward fully understanding the implications of alternative ways to prepare a budget and should motivate future efforts to assess their efficacy in other dimensions.

Chapter 2 describes the budget process and the type of practices typically followed during that process, listing the six budget practices on which the analysis will focus and the ways that they can affect expenditures. Chapter 3 describes the use of these practices across the 50 states from 1988 to 2002. It also describes California's use of these practices in recent history and in comparison to four similar states: Florida, Illinois, New York, and Texas. The core findings of the report are in Chapter 4, which examines the empirical link between practices and two dimensions of government expenditures: total per capita spending and per capita spending on individual budget categories. The last chapter draws some conclusions and elaborates on the policy implications of the findings.

2. Budget Practices with Potential Spending Implications

Identifying a relationship between budget practices and government expenditures requires a description of how different budget management approaches and tools affect the use of resources across government agencies and programs. Much can be learned from knowledge of how the budget process develops and which actors are involved. This chapter uses this approach to identify six budget practices with potential fiscal implications; these are described in the last part of this chapter along with their relationship to expenditures.

The Budget Timeline

Describing the typical budget timeline helps to underscore common budget practice elements across states and, most important, to identify differences that potentially affect expenditures. Singling out such practices is crucial because budgeting is a complex enterprise that requires effort and coordination among several government entities. Even though only the executive and legislative branches are involved in planning the vast majority of public spending, there is room for variation in the tools or procedures each branch uses to develop or approve the funding decisions that constitute the budget.[1]

Approval of a budget usually signifies both the end of a budget cycle and the immediate beginning of the next one. Budget cycle timelines are easily divisible into three broad stages (Figure 2.1). The first includes actions within the primary domain of executive power. During this stage, the administration—through its budget office—provides agencies with instructions to develop their budget requests. Agencies then have a period of time to prepare their funding requests, typically supplementing them with information required by the instructions and additional supporting

[1] It is common for the judicial branch to follow its own budgeting process. In some states, the legislature's spending plan also follows separate procedures independent of the executive power.

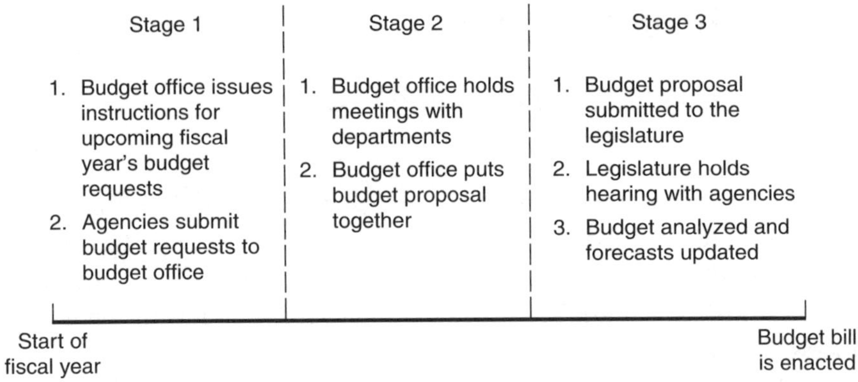

Figure 2.1—A Canonical Budget Timeline

materials of their choice. At the end of this stage, agencies submit their final budget requests to the executive budget office.

In the second stage, the budget office revises and processes the information in the budget requests. Often, the budget office holds meetings with individual agencies for clarification or presentation of supplemental information. The procedures within this stage remain mostly under control of the executive branch through the budget office, but in some cases the legislature participates actively in the development of the budget proposal.[2] After approving, rejecting, or amending all agency budget requests, the budget office consolidates them into a final budget proposal.

Next, the administration presents its budget proposal to the public and the legislature, starting the third and last stage of the budget process. At this point, legislative committees and staffs, as well as a variety of bipartisan, nonpartisan, or joint executive-legislative entities, analyze the budget proposal. During the sessions devoted to budgetary discussions, most legislatures also receive public input or testimony from nongovernmental stakeholders. In addition, some states revise their revenue and caseload forecasts and make them available for the legislature in an effort to gain a more accurate assessment of the state's overall fiscal

[2]The most noteworthy example is Texas, where its Legislative Budget Board—a joint Assembly and Senate Committee—actively participates in the preparation of the budget proposal.

situation and potential demand for services. After the legislature approves the budget—usually incorporating some changes—it ends this stage with the enactment of the budget bill. Enactment can be delayed in states where the governor has the power to veto budget items. In such cases, any disagreement is either resolved through the veto or overridden by specific voting requirements in the legislature—usually a two-thirds vote. After enactment, a new budgeting cycle begins in states with an annual budget process; in states with biennial budgets, the process starts a year later.

This sequence highlights the five principal participants in the budget process (Table 2.1).[3] First are government agencies, the most basic level of the executive branch. Their role in designing and implementing government programs puts them in a position to better understand and measure the need for the services and programs they provide as well as their own outputs and outcomes. The second and third major players are the governor and the budget office. The budget office plays a critical role by providing general guidelines and instructions and communicating the governor's policy objectives in the development of the budget proposal.

Table 2.1

Participants in the Budget Process, by Stage

Stage	Participants
1	Governor
	Budget office
	Government agencies
2	Budget office
	Government agencies
	Legislature
3	Legislature
	Government agencies
	Governor
	Budget analysts

[3]State controllers and auditors often have roles in the budgeting process. However, their roles differ across states and defy consistent classification and, hence, an expected function in shaping expenditures. For this reason, they are excluded from the analysis.

This proposal document also serves as the primary mechanism to communicate the administration's priorities to the fourth budgeting actor: the legislature. The main budgeting function of the legislative branch consists of its evaluation of how the executive budget proposal addresses particular policy objectives and service needs. For this, the legislature often relies on analysis by the fifth actor in the budgeting process: organizations that assess the proposals and give an opinion about the funding levels and some of their policy implications. These organizations can take several forms: bipartisan, bicameral, joint executive-legislative, nonpartisan, or a combination of forms.

We now outline how the budget practices followed by these participants could shape the government's spending decisions.

Links Between Budget Practices and Expenditures

Budget practices do not impose restrictions on fiscal outcomes. Instead, they are the steps and tools that each participant in the budget process uses to carry out its budgetary functions. The budget practices these actors adopt and follow also shape the interaction among them and affect the information with which they work and the time when they access or communicate such information to other participants.

Underlying the premise of a relationship between the adoption of some budget practices and government expenditures is the idea that better management in government can lead to a better assessment of taxpayer demand for different services and programs and of the resources available to provide them. In addition, the availability of this information contributes to better informed voters, who can use it to modify their level of support for government programs.

Identifying how every budget practice contributes to these goals can be a daunting task. Budgeting is a multistage process consisting of numerous practices that cover diverse aspects, from personnel administration to provision of policy guidelines to allotment of appropriated funds. Some of these practices apply to the internal operation of government agencies, and others help establish the relationship and communication between the executive and legislative branches of government during the budgeting process.

Although it is equally conceivable that all practices influence funding decisions in some way or that some practices are irrelevant to expenditures, some of them might have stronger links to spending decisions than others. Among those with the weakest relationship with expenditures are practices related to the length of the process, the timing within the calendar year, or synchronization of the state's budget cycles with the federal fiscal year. By contrast, other practices are more clearly related to an administration's objectives and policies in general and its fiscal policy in particular. One function that budget practices can play is the direct communication of the administration's goals through specific instructions on procedures, policies, and financial objectives or constraints. To the extent that such instructions impose financial criteria restricting agencies' budget requests, or remind them of particular budget rules applicable to the state, they can shape the size of the resulting budget.

Budget practices can also affect the timing at which budget participants have access to particular pieces of information, potentially influencing funding decisions. It is likely that at the beginning of each stage of the budget process, the amount and nature of the information available on programs, caseload and revenue assumptions, and justification for requested funds differ, affecting the context in which budget participants discuss funding proposals. Such changes in reference points can be especially relevant when information is transmitted from one branch of government to another.

Finally, the amount and particular nature of the available information shape budget decisions. The best-known example of this relationship is incremental line-item budgeting. At the core of this system—followed by all states in one way or another—is the principle that when the new budget is being prepared, previous funding constitutes a baseline for future budget allocations. Other information to justify funding decisions includes revenue forecasts, caseload estimates, or the expected effect of federal regulations and requirements on certain programs. Depending on its nature, additional information justifies particular funding levels to programs and agencies and might change the likelihood of modifications to and approval of budget requests.

As mentioned above, budget processes consist of numerous practices and to identify those that conform to these considerations, a consistent account of the budget processes in the states is needed. Fortunately, a series of surveys conducted by the National Association of State Budget Officers (NASBO) and the National Council of State Legislatures (NCSL) provide an overview of the most commonly used budget practices in the country. Using the information contained in these surveys, this report identifies the following six budget practices that could affect government spending:[4]

Funding Targets

This practice takes place at the outset of the budget process. Setting funding targets means that agencies are instructed to abide by specific numerical targets when preparing their funding requests. These targets establish a reference point to determine the size of the budget. When publicly available, funding targets can also serve as an oversight mechanism that allows comparisons between the original budget requests, the budget submitted to the legislature, and the amended and approved spending plan. Insofar as the numerical targets are binding and make their way into the final budget, government spending is likely to be lower when this practice is followed. However, funding targets could also establish a baseline or minimum expenditure requirement for budget requests, in which case government spending is likely to increase where funding targets apply.

Legislative Access to Budget Requests

In some instances, the legislature can access and review agencies' budget requests at the same time as the executive budget office does. This marks a distinction from a situation where the legislature does not participate in the budgeting process until the third stage, when it receives, reviews, and approves the executive budget proposal. The time at which the legislature acquires this information is relevant because the budget proposal consists of requests that are approved in their original form but will not include those that were modified or rejected by the budget office.

There are several arguments as to why this practice could affect spending levels. When they can review these budget requests, legislators

[4]NASBO primarily tracks the role of the executive branch in the budget process and NCSL focuses on legislative processes. For more details on the surveys and the data within, see Appendix A.

with a stake in particular programs might try to ensure that the requested amounts, if not more, are granted to programs related to their constituencies. This practice is a good example of how the starting point of budgeting discussions could affect the outcome in later stages of the process and relates to the idea that outcomes in legislative discussions depend on how the legislative agenda—in this case the budget proposal—compares to the status quo—e.g., the set of previous appropriations, in the case of incremental budgeting systems (Romer and Rosenthal, 1979; Mackay and Weaver, 1983). In particular, without legislative access to budget requests, the initial agenda for legislative budget discussions is the executive budget proposal, which includes only those budget requests that have been approved or modified by the executive power and excludes the rejected ones. By contrast, with legislative access before the budget proposal is prepared, the agenda consists of the entire set of requests, whether or not they are approved by the budget office (and incorporated in the budget proposal).

The effect of this practice on expenditures will depend on how these alternative agendas differ from voters' or legislators' preferences. One plausible effect stems from the idea that legislators have incomplete information on their constituents' preferences (Matsusaka, 1992) and so, therefore, to the extent that budget requests accurately reflect the need for particular programs, legislative access reduces this information gap, enabling the legislature to approve expenditures better aligned with those needs. Alternatively, the information contained in budget requests could underscore differences in the priorities of the executive and legislative branches and could tilt the outcome of the bargaining process in favor of the legislators' particular constituencies. In these cases, it is unclear whether legislative access increases or decreases expenditures or only induces a redistribution of funds across programs.

Performance Measurement

Government agencies engage in performance measurement if they develop metrics on their various programs' outcomes and outputs and track their progress relative to specific benchmarks. The particular measures differ by type of agency and program, but examples include test scores for education, recidivism rates for corrections, and prevented health problems for human services, among many others. Performance measures are retrospective in nature and contrast with the universally used—and by definition, prospective—caseload projections.[5] This practice is primarily followed by individual government agencies but could also result from a statewide policy aimed at better monitoring government services.

Performance measurement could affect expenditures by simply requiring additional resources to measure agencies' outcomes and outputs, including more personnel and the additional capacity necessary to catalogue, classify, and store the resulting data. This increase in expenditures could be temporary, since additional resources would be necessary only at the first stages of the system's implementation.

Performance measurement could also affect expenditures through its oversight mechanism. When performance measures are made public, they contribute to the transparency of the budget process. This in turn informs not only the participants in the budget process but also other stakeholders in the general public, enhancing trust in government and increasing the range of spending acceptable to voters (Alt, Dreyer-Lassen, and Skilling, 2001). Alternatively, increased oversight of government activities through publicly available performance measures could reveal ineffectiveness in certain programs and, in turn, increase resistance to devoting resources to them.

Performance Management

The information that results from measuring agencies' performance often leads to other practices. One of them is the use of performance information by government agencies as a tool to both manage their budget allocations and establish priorities. This could lead to better-informed resource allocation within their own programs and help them develop and optimize their future funding requests. For example, if an agency officer observes that actual performance in some programs is far from its expected goals, he or she could issue directives that put programs back on track or that reallocate resources from some programs into others. The magnitude of this effect will depend on the frequency with which

---

[5]However, both types of measures are not mutually exclusive, as future goals can certainly be correlated with the expected demand for a particular government service.

performance is measured and the degree of budgetary flexibility that agency officers have. Another possibility is the use of performance measures as an input to plan future budget requests. The relationship between this practice and government expenditures could be weak, since the actual use of performance management might not always be reflected in an agency's budget requests. Even if it were, it is the budget office that makes the final decisions on budget requests.

Performance Budgeting

Performance measures can also be used to justify decisions on how total agency budgets will be allocated. This contrasts with the widespread incremental budgeting method, which uses previous levels of funding or of services as the reference point for funding allocations. It is important to note that the two methods are not necessarily mutually exclusive, since performance budgeting and previous funding levels can be combined to rationalize budget decisions. Performance budgeting also provides a mechanism for the public to oversee the results of government activities, increasing the transparency of its operations.

It is important to distinguish performance budgeting from performance management. The former is a tool to help determine the amount of funds allocated to agencies or programs. The latter is a tool for making decisions within programs and agencies, regardless of whether such allocations were made using performance or incremental budgeting. For example, a documented decrease in recidivism (performance measurement) could be used to justify a policy decision that rehabilitation programs are successful and thus require continuous funding (performance budgeting). Once those funds are received by the corrections agency, its head can decide how to allocate them among all programs contributing to reduced recidivism, judging by the programs' performance throughout the fiscal year, and shape future budget requests (performance management).

Both the executive and legislative branches can engage in performance budgeting. Any available performance measures can inform the budget office's proposed allocation of funds. In such cases, both the performance information and the resulting proposed allocations constitute the legislature's starting point for budgetary discussions. Furthermore, the legislature can also use performance measures to justify its decisions to approve, deny, or modify budget items. Thus, performance budgeting can take place at the second or third stages of the budgeting process.

Performance budgeting could relate to expenditures in two ways. First, evidence of underperformance relative to prespecified goals could be interpreted (by either branch of government) as evidence of inadequate funding. In such cases, performance budgeting could fuel spending in particular programs or areas, thus contributing to larger budgets. A second possibility arises if performance measures provide evidence of program ineffectiveness or redundancy. This situation could prompt the elimination of certain functions, with a corresponding reduction in expenditures. Of course, it is also possible that performance budgeting displays no tangible link to expenditures. For example, if performance measures reveal redundancy in some programs and lead to their elimination, the resources freed by this process could be reassigned to other programs rather than being used to reduce funding. Alternatively, budget participants might just not see a clear link between performance information and spending. Either case would leave expenditures unaffected.

Mid-Session Budget Revisions

In all states, there is a period of several months between the submission of the proposed budget and its final approval by the legislature.[6] During this time, the administration can gather information on new economic developments and change its projections on various determinants of the proposed budget, such as tax revenues and caseloads. This provides the executive branch with an opportunity to update its original budget and put the new one under legislative consideration. Even if the executive does not submit a revised budget, when new budget numbers are made public, it gives the legislature the opportunity to adjust its assessment of funding needs.

Mid-session revisions take place during the third stage of the budget process and can change the frame for discussions and final approval. They provide information that helps the adoption of realistic budgets. The final effect of this practice on the size of the budget depends on the direction to which the revisions point. For example, a downward revision

[6] This period, of course, differs by state.

of revenues could restrain spending. Expenditures could be lower than in a state without these revisions. By contrast, if revisions indicate a surge in revenues or caseload, expenditures could increase. However, it is also possible that with a better assessment of the magnitude of new economic conditions, states would adjust their spending in line with the new expected budgetary realities and not overspend.

These six practices fit the criteria for potentially influencing expenditures by three interactions: direct communication of budget policies, the framing of budget discussions through the timing of information disclosure and the ensuing changes in reference points for budgetary discussions, and the provision of additional data to inform budget decisions (Table 2.2). They also offer a glimpse into the numerous procedures involved in budgeting, all of which differ across states.

In sum, changing some budget practices could improve government management and increase the efficiency of its operations, translating into lower spending levels. This was most recently underscored by the California Performance Review's assessment of the state's budgetary process (California Performance Review, 2004), and other states such as Florida (Office of Program Policy Analysis and Government Accountability, 1997) and Oregon (Advisory Committee on Government Performance and

Table 2.2

Budget Practices with Potential Effects on Expenditures

	Stage in the Budgeting Process	Government Branch	Main Budgetary Function
Funding targets	1	Executive	Provide instructions
Legislative access to requests	2	Legislative	Frame discussions
Performance measurement	1	Executive	Accountability
Performance management	1	Executive	Inform requests
Performance budgeting	2, 3	Executive/legislative	Inform allocations
Mid-session revisions	3	Executive/legislative	Inform allocations

Accountability, 2004) have made similar arguments when implementing reforms to their budgeting processes. The following chapter examines the particular practices in California, their recent evolution, and how they compare to the practices in similar states.

3. Budget Practices Across the Nation and in California

This chapter reviews the use of the six budget practices across the nation and in California. It relies on several published surveys to describe the evolution of these practices from 1988 through 2002 and finds that these practices have been widely used throughout the country. Finally, the chapter focuses on the use of these practices in California, putting them in context by providing a brief historical account of how the state has adopted some of them and comparing them to those currently followed by Florida, Illinois, New York, and Texas.

The National Landscape

As of 2002, the most commonly used practice was performance measures, with 38 states using this practice in at least one government area (Table 3.1). This widespread use of performance measurement results from the fact that in many states, the focus on performance is not a statewide coordinated effort but rather one that individual agencies develop on their own. As a result, some states have performance measures in at least one government area but not in all. Requiring that all government areas develop performance measures is a stricter criterion that often captures whether a state follows a formal performance budgeting process, as in Texas. Using this criterion indicates that 29 states measure performance for agencies in all government areas.

Similarly, performance management in at least one government area was used slightly more frequently than performance budgeting (24 states with the former, 21 with the latter). If we focus on the stricter requirement that agencies in all government areas develop and use the performance information in this way, performance management and budgeting are used equally across states. Funding targets and legislative access were also commonly used, with 34 states following the former and 30 allowing the latter. The least-used practice in 2002 was the mid-session revision, with only 14 states employing it.

Table 3.1

The Number of States Implementing Budget Practices, 2002

Funding targets	34
Legislative access	30
Performance measurement	
In at least one government area	38
In all government areas	*29*
Performance management[a]	
In at least one government area	24
In all government areas	*19*
Performance budgeting	
In at least one government area	21
In all government areas	*19*
Mid-session revision	14

SOURCES: National Association of State Budget Offices, National Council of State Legislatures, Crain and O'Roark (2004).

[a]Data for 2002 are unavailable; the figures reflect the use of performance management in 2000.

States often embark on formal and informal experiments to modify their budget processes to improve government operations. These reforms often follow recurrent patterns, with a particular method being in vogue for some time, eventually losing popularity, and regaining it years later (Burns and Lee, 2004).

Adoption patterns between 1988 and 2002 suggest that practices linked to the interaction between the legislative and executive powers experienced fewer changes in their adoption than those practices involving directives issued by the state governor (Figure 3.1).[1] Two practices illustrate the role of these constraints best: funding targets and legislative access.

The use of funding targets increased significantly in the mid-1980s after a long period in the late 1970s when they were used by only eight

[1]These different patterns might stem from the relative ease with which practices are adopted, reformed, or abandoned. In turn, this is partially a function of their origin in law by statute, mandate, or constitution. Unfortunately, the available data do not allow distinguishing these important features of budget practices.

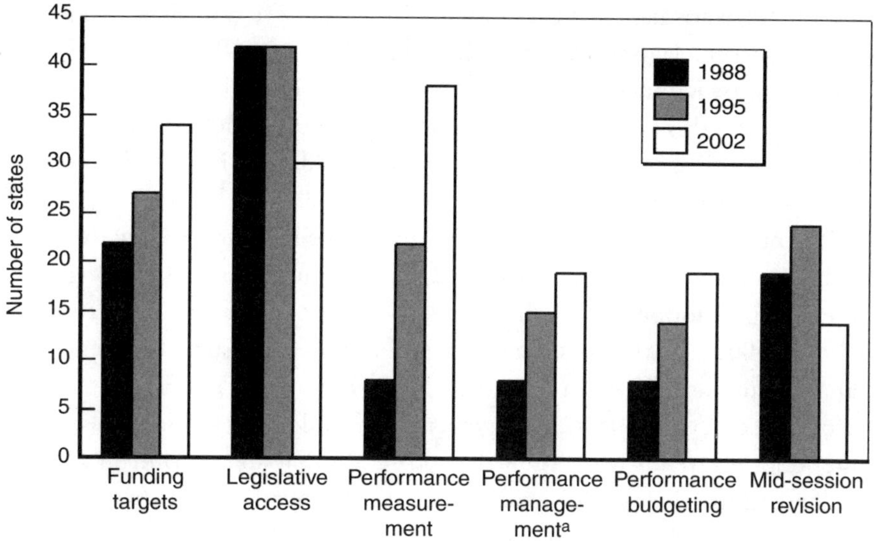

[a]Observation for 2002 corresponds to 2000 because data on this practice were unavailable for 2002.

Figure 3.1—The Adoption Patterns of Budget Practices Across the Nation, Selected Years

states: Alaska, Colorado, Maryland, Massachusetts, South Carolina, Vermont, Wisconsin, and Wyoming. By 1986 and 1987, 40 states were using them, possibly as a response to the economic fluctuations thataffected government revenues in those years and that made spending restrictions necessary. Only 22 states used funding targets in 1988 but, since then, the number has remained stable, although some states instituted them and then later suspended them.[2]

Thirty states allowed legislative access throughout the 1988–2002 period but this was a decline from previous years. California has never

[2]It is unclear why the number of states using funding targets dropped so abruptly from 1987 to 1988. One possibility is that some states adopted other reforms that helped them cope with revenue shortfalls. Another possibility is that these conditions were perceived as transitory by state budget offices and that funding targets were used only as a temporary measure for one or two years, especially in states with tax and expenditure limits, where a surge in revenues prompted sizable tax rebates.

allowed all government agencies to share the information in their budget requests with the legislature, and neither have Illinois or Pennsylvania.[3] Massachusetts, Minnesota, and New Jersey are among a handful of states that once used this practice but have stopped. Among the states that have adopted legislative access in recent times are Florida and New York; it has been in place in Texas and Oregon since at least 1976.

The number of states developing performance measures has increased steadily from six in 1977 to 38 in 2002, but the number of states using these measures for budgeting dropped slightly from a peak of 26 in 2000 to 19 in 2002. The trend in the use of performance measures for agency management has followed a similar pattern. These three practices—performance measurement, management, and budgeting—also display the same adoption trends when the stricter criterion that all government areas develop and use their performance measures is applied. This expansion follows from another trend in recent years: to provide the budgeting process with more tools to increase the rationality of resource allocation and to enhance government accountability (Melkers and Willoughby, 1998).

The mid-session budget revision has undergone significant changes in its use in recent years. The number of states making updates on revenue and caseload projections during the legislative session increased from 19 in 1988 to 27 in 2000 and later dropped to only 14 in 2002, the lowest number in this period. Connecticut, Delaware, Iowa, Kansas, Louisiana, Maine, Massachusetts, Minnesota, New Jersey, New York, Oregon, Rhode Island, Vermont, Virginia, and Washington abandoned this practice between 2000 and 2002, whereas Illinois, Maryland, and Texas adopted it. It is also worth mentioning that from 1988 to 2002, in almost half of the states following this practice, an agency different from the one in charge

[3]However, this does happen in very particular cases. For example, the Board of Regents of the University of California typically presents a budget request in the fall. Since the Assembly Speaker is a member of this board, it is likely that the legislature knows of such requests before seeing the governor's proposal. Nevertheless, given government officials' responses to the NCSL, this does not seem to be a generalized practice in California. I thank Daniel Mitchell for pointing out this example.

of the original forecasts (usually the budget office) had responsibility for making these revisions.[4]

In sum, states' budget processes have evolved through time. Part of the pattern observed in budget processes across the nation is a continuous adoption and suspension of budget practices. The history of these changes understandably differs across states for various reasons. Identifying California's changes in budget practices through time and relative to states facing similar circumstances should provide some insights into why the state has chosen to follow some budget practices and not others.

The Development of California's Current Budget Practices

California's current budgeting process was shaped early in the 20th century following the ideas of the Progressive Era reformers, who sought to create strong forms of government by implementing tools such as standardized accounting and reporting practices. The state's executive budget resulted as a response to the then-prevalent "bureaucratic feudalism," when most departments' own appropriation bills passed at different times. Reformers thought it imperative that the appropriation bills be related to each other, to projected revenues, and to larger social objectives and policies.

California adopted the core of its executive budgeting process in 1922. From the beginning, it required that the governor submit a unified and balanced biennial budget (changed to annual shortly afterward) accompanied by a budget bill.[5] Such requirements made the executive's spending proposal the starting point for budgetary deliberations in the legislature, setting the agenda for the allocation of resources in the state.

The California Department of Finance was created in 1927 and marked the beginning of the development of California's budget practices. The

---

[4]It is important to keep in mind that these changes in the use of mid-session revisions could arise if, as in the case of California, these updates are not required by statute or law. However, what is important for the analysis is whether or not states follow this practice, regardless of its compulsory nature.

[5]The exact definition of "balanced" is unclear, however.

legislature created the Legislative Analyst's Office (LAO) in 1942 to provide nonpartisan budget and policy advice to the legislature for its discussions with the executive about the budget. The legislature then created the Commission on California State Government Organization and Economy in 1962—also known as the Little Hoover Commission—with the goal of promoting efficiency and effectiveness in state programs. The Commission on State Finance—a joint commission that included the director of the Department of Finance, the state treasurer and controller, and members of the legislature—was created in 1979 to provide quarterly revenue and expenditure forecasts.[6]

With few exceptions, agencies' budget requests in California have always been confidential and therefore the legislature does not have access to them until after it receives the governor's proposed budget. The Department of Finance explicitly reminds agencies of this requirement in its budget preparation guidelines.[7]

Although the lack of legislative access has been immutable in California's budgeting process, the state has changed its use of other practices. The Department of Finance did not provide government agencies with specific funding targets for their budget requests until the 1988–1989 budget. In that year, the department justified its change because it was projecting that revenues would exceed the state's appropriation limit.[8] California continued to use funding targets until 1998, but the reasons for imposing them differed throughout the years. From 1990 to 1995, consecutive declines in revenues and an uncertain economic environment prompted funding targets that ranged from actual reductions of as much as 10 percent to increases of no more than 2 percent. From 1996 to 1998, the uncertain effect of federal welfare reform on California's programs added

[6]The commission was dissolved in 1993 as a consequence of that year's tight fiscal circumstances.

[7]For example, the department's Budget Letter 05-33 issued in December 2005 reminds agencies that "budget decisions are confidential until after the Governor's Budget is released on or before January 10, 2006."

[8]California voters approved Proposition 4 in 1979, which limits the growth in state and local government appropriation from taxes to no more than the annual changes in population and the lesser of the U.S. Consumer Price Index or personal income. The combination of this limit and a substantial increase in general fund revenues had caused the state's first-ever (and to this date, only) refund to taxpayers in 1987.

to the arguments to limit agencies' funding requests. The Department of Finance did not specify funding targets again until fiscal years 2003 through 2005 but did not require them in preparation for the 2006 budget.

California had brief experiences with alternative budgeting systems, such as zero-based budgeting in the early 1970s and undertook its most serious attempt to date in 1993 with the introduction of performance-based budgeting in selected agencies.[9] The economic downturn of the early 1990s triggered this experiment, which was implemented as an evaluation pilot program in four state departments—General Services, Consumer Affairs, Parks and Recreation, and the California Conservation Corps. The goals of the pilot programs were to find more cost-effective ways to deliver government services through strategic planning, the development of performance measures, and their use in management and budgeting decisions.

The pilots ended in 1996 because, according to reviews by the California Department of Finance (1996) and the California Legislative Analyst's Office (1996), the cost to agencies of maintaining incremental and performance-based budgeting systems simultaneously was high, and the links between performance measures and budgeting decisions were unclear. Nevertheless, some agencies (e.g., the Department of Parks and Recreation) still keep track of some performance indicators, although they are rarely used in the current budgeting process.

Currently, California's budgeting cycle starts in July of each calendar year, immediately after the enactment of its most recent budget. At this point, the Department of Finance distributes its budget letters to government agencies. These contain policy and financial guidelines based on the governor's priorities and the department's forecasts of revenue and relevant procurement costs. During the most recent budget cycle—in preparation for the 2006–2007 budget cycle—the budget letters contained

---

[9]Zero-based budgeting results from the idea that each year, the achievements of agencies and programs, as well as the necessity to maintain them in following years, must be evaluated from scratch. The goal of this system is to make programs compete for limited funding based on performance and priorities rather than on prior years' funding, as the incremental budgeting process does. Performance-based budgeting is described in Chapter 2.

no explicit indication of funding targets (either floors or ceilings) for agencies' budget requests.

By September or October, agencies submit their budget baselines and requests along with any other relevant information—mostly their caseload estimates—to the Department of Finance. From October to December, the department meets with officials from individual agencies and, if necessary, asks for more information to justify their requests. California's legislature has no formal channel to participate in the budgeting discussion during this stage. In fact, as described above, budget letters explicitly forbid agencies to disclose the information contained in their budget requests until after the submission of the governor's budget to the legislature. Thus, except in the case of some independent entities (e.g., the University of California or the courts), legislative access is not practiced in California.

The last stage of California's budgeting process starts on or after January 10 of each year when the governor submits a proposed budget. Discussion of the budget with the legislature follows several smaller steps within this stage. First, the governor's proposed budget is subject to exhaustive analysis. The LAO is a key participant at this point.[10] Legislative discussions start after the LAO issues its analysis of the budget and recommendations in February. For the following two months, the legislature holds public hearings and receives testimony from agencies' staff, the Department of Finance, and diverse stakeholders from the general public.

The discussions at these hearings revolve around caseload assumptions and justifications for requested increases in funding relative to previous years' allocations. Some agencies develop and provide performance measures, in particular, descriptions and quantifications of their objectives of the previous fiscal year, as well as their progress in achieving those stated goals. However, there is little indication that performance measures are commonly used to make budgeting decisions. For example, the Assembly and Senate discussions held between March 2 and May 21, 2005, on 2005–2006 budget items in Health and Human Services, Public Safety, Transportation, and General Government allocations barely made reference

[10]The LAO is appointed by the Assembly and Senate's Joint Legislative Budget Committee to provide objective and nonpartisan analysis and recommendations for changes in the budget plan.

Table 3.4

Selected Characteristics of California and Comparison States, 2002

	Population (1,000s)	Nonwhite (%)	Age 65+ (%)	Age <18 (%)	Foreign-Born (%)	Size of Government (% of Gross State Product)
California	34,988	33	11	28	27	9
Florida	16,678	21	17	24	18	9
Illinois	12,587	24	12	25	13	8
New York	19,165	30	13	24	21	9
Texas	21,722	25	10	29	15	9

SOURCES: Bureau of Economic Analysis and Bureau of the Census.

comparisons for each practice instead of following the timeline in each state. The comparisons should not be interpreted as exhaustive or prescriptive but rather as providing a benchmark from states admittedly unique in many other dimensions.

In this group, Illinois and New York used funding targets in their executive budget guidelines at the start of the budgeting cycle in 2005 (Table 3.5). Although funding targets have been common in recent years in Illinois, New York has used them more sporadically, in effect in 1986 and 1987 and abandoned shortly afterward, but used again since 2002.

Table 3.5

Budget Practices in Selected States, 2005

	California	Florida	Illinois	New York	Texas
Funding targets			X	X	
Legislative access		X			X
Performance measurement		X	X	X	X
Performance management		X	X	X	X
Performance budgeting		X	X	X	X
Mid-session revision	X	X	X		X

SOURCE: Direct contact with states' budget offices and legislatures' websites.

Florida's government agencies have not been required to meet any particular funding target in their legislative budget requests in several years. This was reflected in surveys by NASBO, which indicate that Florida used explicit financial targets only during the late 1980s and early 1990s. Similarly, although Texas's Legislative Budget Board informs agencies of the limit for total state expenditures, this does not translate into specific financial targets for their requests.

Legislative access to agencies' budget requests before the executive budget is developed seems to be related to the degree of involvement that legislatures have in developing the budget proposal. Texas provides a good illustration of this relationship. In Texas, the Executive Budget Office and the Legislative Budget Board prepare budget guidelines jointly. They also simultaneously receive agencies' Legislative Authorization Requests, but the Legislative Budget Board prepares the budget plan that is ultimately sent for legislative scrutiny.

In Florida, although the legislature is not as deeply involved in the first stages of its budgeting process, government agencies submit their Legislative Budget Requests simultaneously to the budget office and to the appropriations committees in both legislative chambers. In contrast to California, neither Illinois nor New York explicitly prohibits government agencies from sharing the content of their budget requests before submission of the executive budget plan but both states report that this practice has not been used recently.

Another difference from California is other states' development of performance measures by agencies and their use for management or budgeting. Texas's use of long-term plans that establish goals for each agency and program is recognized as the most complete and advanced performance management and budgeting system in the country (Liner, Dusenbury, and Vinson, 2000). In fact, each line item in its budget bill is accompanied by an average of two output or outcome performance measures that justify the allocation of funds.[12] Florida implemented a

[12]For example, in its budget for the 2004–2005 biennium, Texas's Commission on Jail Standards states its goal ("establish reasonable minimum standards for the operation of jails"), defines outcomes by which achievement toward the goal is measured ("number of jails achieving compliance," and "percentage of jails with management-related deficiencies"), and links strategies/appropriations ($300 million to "develop and

performance budgeting system modeled after Texas's in 1996 (Office of Program Policy Analysis and Government Accountability, 1997). The use of performance measures is not as institutionalized or structured in Illinois and New York as it is in Florida and Texas. According to NASBO, to the Illinois Office of Management and Budget, and to New York's Division of the Budget, some agencies in these two states develop performance measures even if they are not legally required to do so. Agencies also decide whether to use performance information for their internal planning only (i.e., performance management) or include it in their budget requests.

Finally, the only state in this group that does not make mid-session revisions to its budget proposal is New York. Florida revises its revenue forecasts at least twice a year but can make further updates when the budget office deems it necessary. Illinois makes quarterly revisions to its revenue projections. Two of these, in February and April, fall within the period of legislative discussions of the budget plan. Texas has a schedule for its revenue projections similar to California's: an initial estimate in January followed by a May revision that falls during the legislative analysis of the budget. However, Texas makes these estimates only every other year because of its biennial budgeting cycle.

Tables 3.3 and 3.5 show that despite the similarities between California and other states in some important socioeconomic dimensions, their budget processes consist of different practices. The contrast is particularly marked between California—where planning and preparation of the budget are dominated by executive power—and Texas—where the legislature plays a very active role in all stages of the budgeting process. Likewise, California does not have a formal system of evaluating agencies' performance to assist management or allocate funds, and Texas's budgeting process relies heavily on performance measures. Finally, Texas follows a biennial budgeting cycle and California develops its budget on a yearly basis.

To understand the fiscal consequences of past and potential future changes to California's budgeting process, it is important to determine to what extent changes in budget practices throughout the country have affected state expenditures. The following chapter undertakes this task.

---

implement a process to inspect, monitor compliance and ensure due process in enforcement of standards for local jails" in 2004) to those outcomes and additional outputs ("number of annual inspections conducted").

4. How Budget Practices Shape State Expenditures

The analysis in this chapter focuses on two dimensions of spending: expenditures per capita and spending by service category. The period of analysis is limited to the years 1988–2000, owing to a lack of information on the use of mid-session revisions before 1988, a frequency of observations on budget practices before 1988 insufficient to identify their relationship with expenditures, and unavailable data on performance management after 2000.

The definition of expenditures follows the Census of Governments categorization and includes current and capital expenditures and state assistance to local governments; it excludes interest on debt, insurance trust fund benefits and payments, and spending on utilities. One disadvantage of using this definition is that the Bureau of the Census does not disaggregate data in a way that allows focusing on general fund expenditures exclusively, although most of them are included in this construct. However, Census data have the crucial advantage of enabling expenditure comparisons across states, which allow meaningful conclusions on the relationship between expenditures and budget practices to be drawn. Also, spending by local governments is not part of the analysis because local governments follow different budgeting processes that do not necessarily incorporate the practices discussed in the previous chapters. Government expenditures, as well as all monetary variables used in the analysis, are deflated with the Consumer Price Index (CPI) and presented in real 2002 dollars per capita.

The data do suggest an association of some budget practices with different levels of state expenditures (Table 4.1). During the period under study, per capita expenditures were $524 lower in states that used legislative access and $170 lower in those that practiced performance management. By contrast, states using the mid-session revision practice had expenditures per capita $386 higher, on average. All these differences are statistically significant. Some differences in government spending by budget practice were not statistically different from zero: expenditures in states using

Table 4.1

Average Total State Expenditures, by Budget Practice (in real per capita dollars)

	Without Practice	With Practice	Difference in Dollars	Percentage Difference
Funding targets	3,151	3,187	36	1
Legislative access*	3,572	3,048	–524	–16
Performance measurement	3,155	3,189	34	1
Performance management*	3,226	3,056	–170	–5
Performance budgeting	3,201	3,109	–92	–3
Mid-session revision*	2,994	3,380	386	12

*Denotes statistically significant difference at the 10 percent level or less.

funding targets or performance measures, which had about $30 per capita higher expenditures, and states using performance budgeting, which had $92 lower per capita expenditures on average.

To determine more precisely the magnitude and significance of effects on government spending, it is necessary to take into account the fact that states can change their practices and that budgets evolve with changes in the state economies, with the demand for public services that those changes entail, and various historical characteristics.

The ideal way to measure the effect of a particular budget practice on a state's budget can be illustrated through the following thought experiment: First, assume that a state's socioeconomic characteristics do not change from one year to the next. Then, change its budget process by either adopting or abandoning one of its budget practices. In this fashion, any resulting change in expenditures can be attributed either to the effects of the budget practice or to mere chance. Unfortunately, experimenting in such a way with a state's budget process is both impractical (the economy cannot be stopped at will) and costly (some consequences may be unintended). However, it is possible to tease out the same type of effects by looking at how expenditures in states that follow a particular budget practice differ from spending levels in states without it. Obviously, this type of comparison has to take into account the fact that not all states are equal: Their population, income levels, demographics, and politics can differ substantially. In turn, these characteristics shape expenditures to a large extent.

The basic framework to correctly carry out this analysis uses multivariate regression. The idea behind this technique is to first account for how the population's preferences for government services and the political process determine government expenditures. After this is done, the remaining differences in spending can be attributed to budget practices or to other unobservable characteristics. The success of this technique depends on incorporating as many observable determinants of government spending as possible. The reason for this is that if an important determinant of spending is excluded, then its effects will be captured by all other variables included in the equation, which will bias the estimates of their effects and relationships with government expenditures. Thus, omitting important determinants of spending affects the conclusions on the magnitude and significance of any other variables, including budget practices.

This technique will provide estimates of the effect of budget practices on expenditures if the adoption of budget practices is independent of the unobserved characteristics that also influence government expenditures. This is a restrictive assumption in practice because it is possible that states with a long-standing tradition of limited government or with an efficiency-oriented political culture are more likely to adopt budget practices that serve those purposes. Moreover, it is common for states to explore the adoption of certain budget practices in times of fiscal difficulties, when expenditures tend to be lower already. Failing to account for these unobserved characteristics that influence both government spending and the use of a particular budget practice will at best provide evidence that expenditures and budget practices are significantly correlated but will reveal nothing about the effect that the latter have on the former.

Fortunately, it is possible to address this issue by first calculating the propensity of a state to adopt a budget practice, as long as some of its observed characteristics do not affect spending directly. This calculation is then used to estimate the effect that a budget practice has on expenditures after accounting for all common observed and unobserved determinants. In the case of budget practices, other states' experiences provide a useful way to get at the causal effects of practices on expenditures. The reason is that states usually analyze what other states have done with a practice and the results they have obtained to evaluate whether to adopt it. At the same time, how other states prepare their budgets is unlikely to determine expenditures in the state considering the adoption of a practice.

Following the standard literature on estimating the determinants of public spending (Bergstrom and Goodman, 1973), the remainder of this chapter applies the two-step multivariate regression technique described above and includes the following variables: personal income, transfers from the federal government, demographic composition of the population, the unemployment rate, the percentage of the population living in metropolitan areas, citizen and government ideology indexes, and a divided government indicator, for cases in which the governor's political party is different from the party in control of both chambers in the state legislature (Table 4.2). In addition, the framework incorporates the possible effects that budget rules such as tax and expenditure limits, gubernatorial line-item veto power, and supermajority requirements for tax increases have on state expenditures. Finally, state characteristics that do not change throughout time (e.g., the size of the state or the fixed costs of implementing new policies) and events that affect all states in the same year (e.g., a national economic recession) are also incorporated into the framework.

Personal income provides a rough estimate of the tax base available to state governments: Higher income levels translate into higher government revenue either through the income tax (where applicable) or through purchases and general economic activities that entail taxation or assessments, such as sales or real estate transactions. The demographic composition by age group, ethnicity, and metropolitan area, together with the unemployment rate, are all associated with the demand for public services such as education, health care, social assistance, and public safety.

The ideology indexes are included to capture the political and ideological determinants of government spending policies. These indexes measure average beliefs on a conservative-to-liberal spectrum and range from 0 (extremely conservative) to 100 (extremely liberal). Both indexes aggregate information from several sources. The first includes interest group ratings of states' members of Congress, most notably Americans for Democratic Action (ADA), Americans for Constitutional Action (ACA),

Table 4.2

The Key Characteristics of States, by Use of Practices, 1988–2000

	With Less Than Four Practices	With at Least Four Practices
State government expenditures	3,174	3,162
Personal income*	26,130	27,185
Transfers from the federal government*	1,792	1,685
% of population age < 18*	26.12	25.69
% of population age > 64	12.43	12.53
% of population nonwhite*	15.07	19.98
% of population in metropolitan areas*	61.68	71.87
Unemployment rate*	5.36	4.98
Citizen ideology index	48.65	48.28
Government ideology index*	50.59	46.70
Divided government (= 1 if yes)	0.60	0.64
Tax/expenditure limits (= 1 if yes)*	0.38	0.64
Line-item veto (= 1 if yes)	0.79	0.83
Supermajority required for tax increases (= 1 if yes)*	0.17	0.31
Number of state-year observations	424	226

NOTE: Monetary variables are in 2002 per capita dollars.

*Denotes statistically significant difference at the 10 percent level or less.

and the American Federation of Labor-Congress of Industrial Organizations' Committee on Political Education (COPE). In addition, they use election returns from congressional races, the party composition of state legislatures, and the party affiliation of governors. Thus, the indexes incorporate information on the partisan control of the two government branches that have budgeting functions and account for differences in ideologies of elected officials within political parties and of the electorate.[1]

The indicator of a divided government is included to incorporate the possibility that political conflict makes agreements on policies more difficult to achieve, including those related to spending decisions. Finally, tax and expenditure limits, the line-item veto, and supermajority requirements for tax increases are included to control for any possible

[1] These indexes were originally developed and constructed by Berry et al. (1998).

correlation between budget rules and budget practices that could blur the estimates of their effects on spending.

Overall Relationships with Total Expenditures

The results of the multivariate regression model corroborate some of the differences suggested by the simple comparison of average expenditures. As expected, the estimated fiscal effect of each budget practice is different from what the comparisons of means suggest because the multivariate analysis takes into account state characteristics that by themselves could increase or decrease the level of state expenditures, such as the size and evolution of the state economy.

Three of the budget practices under study have an association with per capita expenditures that is statistically significant; all of them reduce spending (Figure 4.1). These are funding targets, legislative access, and performance budgeting.

When government agencies must abide by specific funding targets in their budget requests, expenditures are 1.7 percent lower than in states

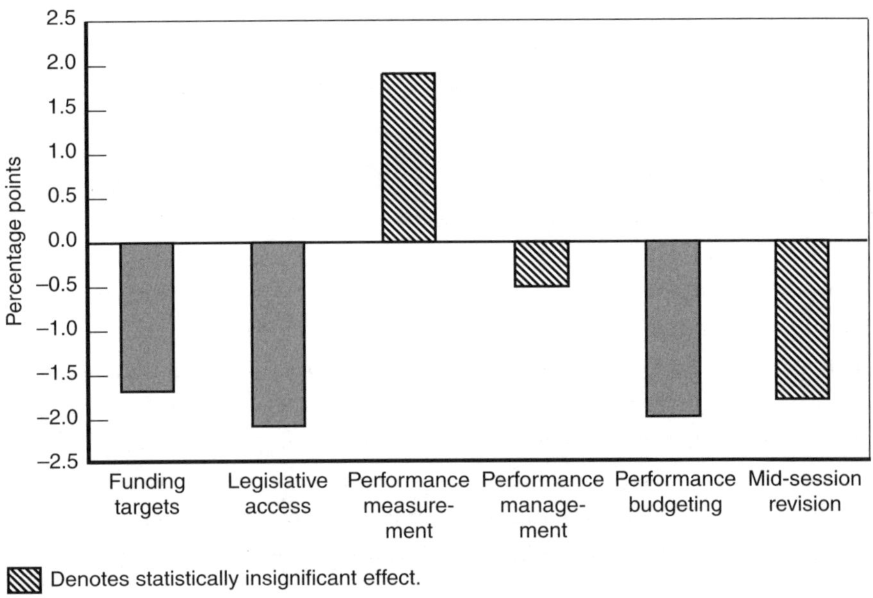

Figure 4.1—The Effects of Budget Practices on State Expenditures per Capita

where government agencies do not follow this guideline. This is consistent with the idea that funding targets are equivalent to expenditure caps for individual agencies: When all agencies are subject to these caps, overall expenditures are reduced as well.

Similarly, legislative access reduces expenditures by 2.1 percent. This finding is consistent with the idea outlined in Chapter 2 that this practice facilitates an early exchange of information between the executive and legislative branches that underscores the differences in their priorities and their assessment of funding needs, fostering a more efficient decisionmaking process. This result might also indicate that legislative involvement in the budgeting process at early stages serves as an oversight mechanism that keeps some of the expenditures proposed by the executive branch in check, especially in areas where legislators' constituencies do not have strong or influential vested interests.

Performance budgeting reduces state government expenditures by 2 percent. This is consistent with the view that performance budgeting can streamline government programs, reduce inefficiencies, and trim costs. The finding, in line with previous findings in the academic literature (Crain and O'Roark, 2004), is also consistent with an allocation of fewer resources to programs or agencies with unsatisfactory performance.

A necessary condition for performance budgeting is the development, maintenance, and updating of a system of performance measures. Developing performance measures in at least one government area increases expenditures by roughly the same amount as the reduction derived from following performance budgeting (1.9%). However, this effect is not statistically significant. Thus, the benefits of performance budgeting are not completely offset by the costs of developing the underlying performance measures. Performance management, the other use of performance measures, is associated with a 0.5 percent reduction in expenditures, but the effect lacks statistical significance.

Finally, the effect of mid-session revisions is to reduce spending by 1.8 percent. The absence of a significant effect could be the consequence of the aggregation of two possible scenarios. The first is when updated forecasts indicate that government resources will be lower than expected. In such cases, a state with mid-session revisions would be able to inform the legislature and adjust expenditures downward. Second, when the forecast on caseload or revenue is adjusted upward, states could increase their spending accordingly. If the forecasts are accurate on average, then reductions and increases in spending balance each other out and render the average effect insignificant.[2]

These estimates capture the average response of government expenditure levels throughout the entire period that an individual budget practice is in effect.[3] It is natural to ask how long it takes for the effects of budget practices on expenditures to materialize and whether they are long-lasting or of short duration. The remainder of this section describes these relationships for the three practices with overall significant effects on expenditures. To do so, it looks at how the relationship between each budget practice and spending changes as a practice remains in effect throughout time in states that adopted each practice at any time after 1988 (the first year that data on mid-session revisions are available) or after 1977 (the first year that data on the rest of the practices are available).[4]

Expenditures are not significantly correlated with funding targets until this practice has been in effect for three to six years (Figure 4.2). After that, there is no significant correlation with spending until after the 15th year in effect, suggesting that a state must maintain this practice over the long run to see any effects.

The relationship between legislative access and total expenditures is significant shortly after the adoption of this practice and remains so more or less consistently through time (Figure 4.3). States that followed this practice for one year during the sample period had no significantly different spending levels, but expenditures in those allowing legislative access for two and up to nine years spent between 3 and 8 percent less. The relationship

---

[2]The negative (albeit statistically insignificant) effect could arise if revisions have an asymmetric effect: Budget participants react more whenever updates reveal "bad times" than when they reveal "good" ones. If this is the case, the negative effect of the practice would reflect the actions taken at the time of the revisions, not a bias of the revisions themselves. Unfortunately, data limitations prevent testing these hypotheses.

[3]In other words, the reader should be cautious not to interpret these estimates as "immediate" or "one-time" effects of a particular practice but instead as a combination of the short- and long-term effects of having a practice in place.

[4]The nature of this analysis does not allow estimating the causal effects of budget practices by year in effect. Thus, the conclusions are valid for the approximate timing of the effects but not for their magnitude. See Appendix B for details.

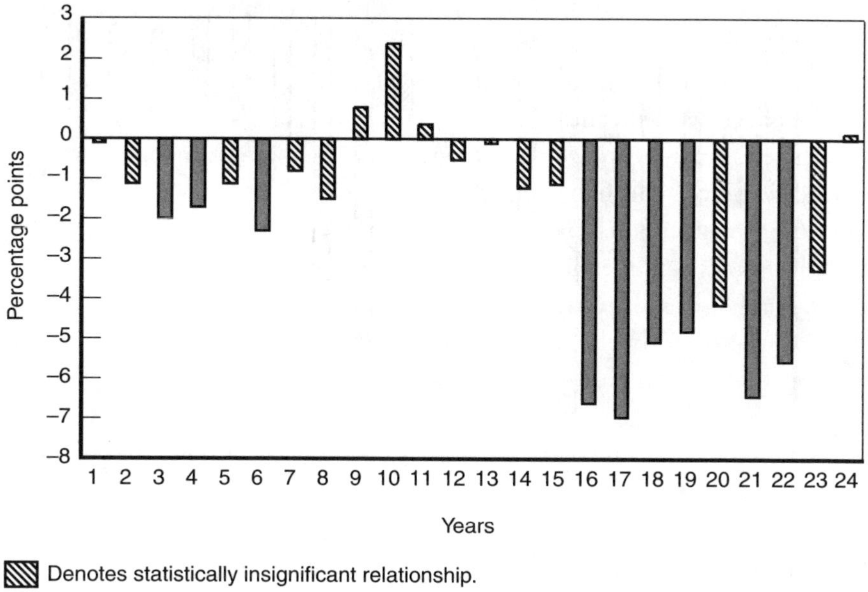

Figure 4.2—The Relationship Between Total Expenditures and Funding Targets, by Years in Effect

between spending and legislative access that has been in place for ten years and longer is of a slightly smaller magnitude, and its statistical significance fades with time. In fact, spending levels in states that have followed legislative access since at least 1977 were no different from spending levels in states without this practice during the period under study.

Government spending exhibited a negative relationship to performance budgeting throughout the years this practice was in effect, although the link was not always statistically significant (Figure 4.5). Total expenditures were up to 3 percent in the first four years after the adoption of this practice but were not significantly different from four to 11 years after. However, spending was significantly lower when performance budgeting had been in place for longer periods of time, in particular for up to 15 years. Such a pattern could arise if lower expenditures result in the beginning from the elimination of redundant programs. Lower spending levels in later years would reflect a shift in government culture as budgeting decisions become based on performance. These findings suggest that the reduced

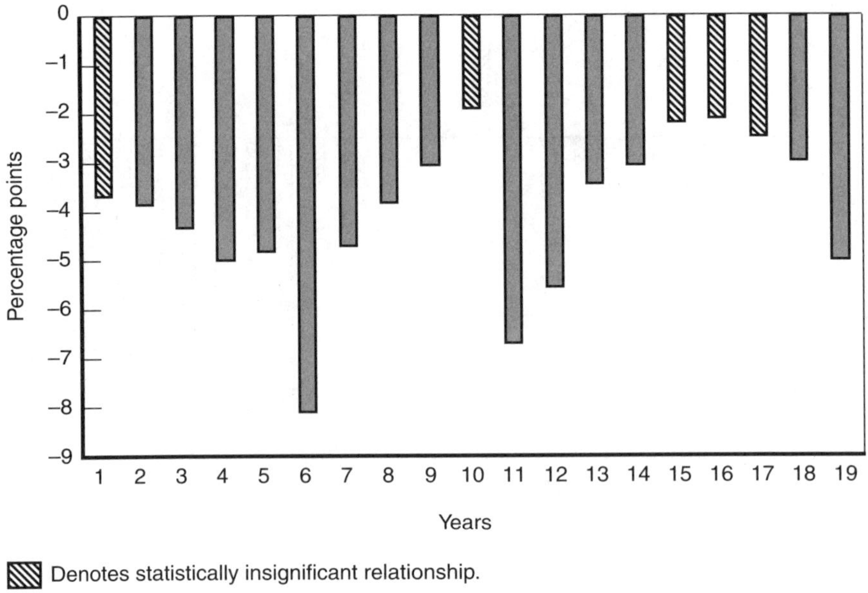

Figure 4.3—The Relationship Between Total Expenditures and Legislative Access, by Years in Effect

expenditures from implementing performance budgeting take time to accrue in their totality.

Budget Practices and Spending Categories

It is conceivable that by changing the level of total state expenditures, budget practices affect spending levels in separate categories differently. Many state programs are strongly influenced either by state constitutional mandates such as education in California or by federal policies in areas such as health and social services. State governments have more freedom in determining spending levels in other categories such as public safety and government administration. The remainder of this chapter examines how the three budget practices with significant effects on total expenditures have a different effect on each type of spending, as classified by the Bureau of the

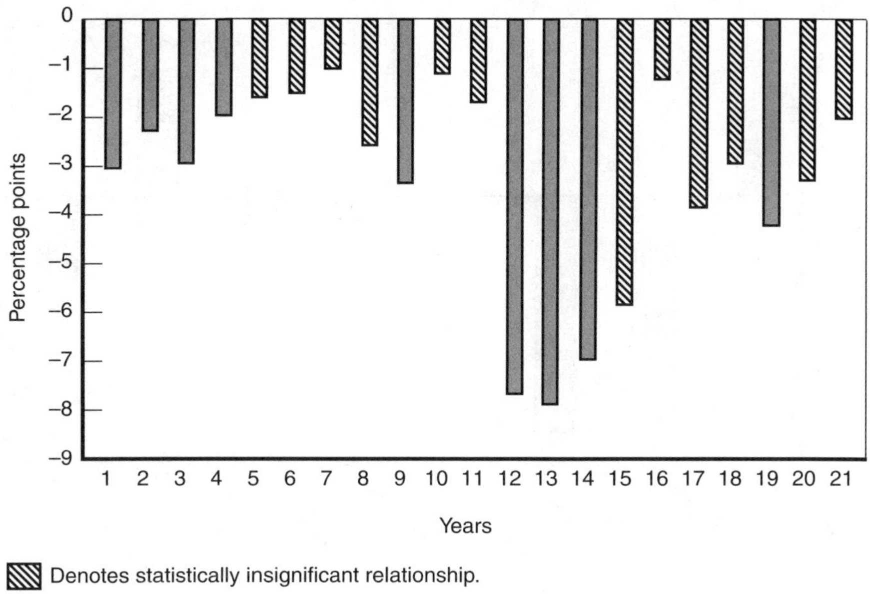

Figure 4.4—The Relationship Between Total Expenditures and Performance Budgeting, by Years in Effect

the Census.[5] Applying the same two-step multivariate regression method as with total expenditures reveals that certain budget practices affect specific spending categories in a way largely consistent with their overall relationship with total expenditures.

Funding Targets

The use of funding targets reduces spending in all categories—although not always at statistically significant levels—except for government administration and social services (Figure 4.5). A possible explanation for their positive relationship with social services is that many of these expenditures are linked to federal welfare programs that require

[5]In what follows, the category "government administration" equals the sum of the Census categories "general government" and "other government." It also excludes spending on the legislative and judicial branches because many states follow budget processes different from the one examined in this report.

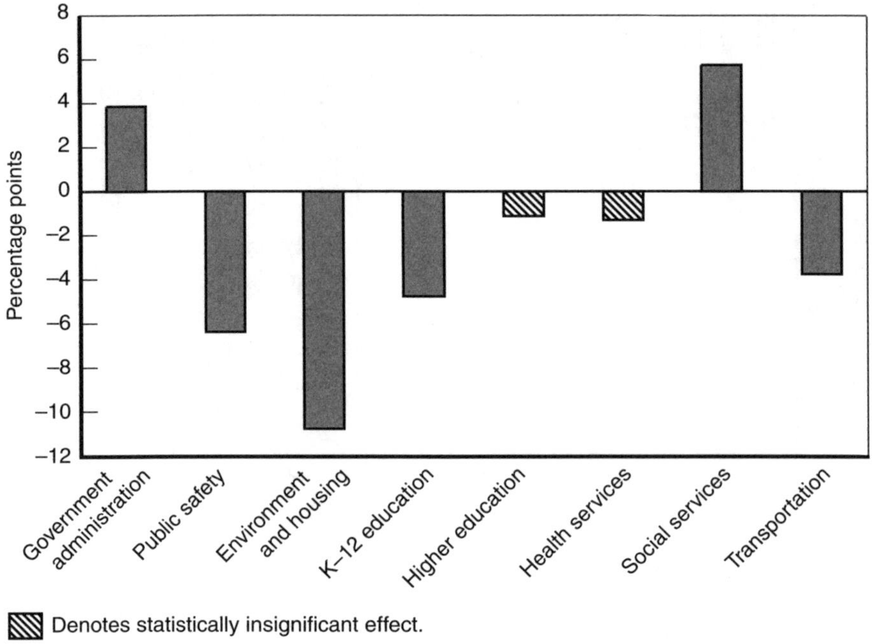

Figure 4.5—The Effect of Funding Targets on State Expenditures, by Spending Category

that states maintain specific minimum spending levels.[6] Thus, the funding target could be interpreted as a spending floor rather than as a ceiling. The federal component could also be the reason behind the lack of significance in the relationship between funding targets and health expenditures, a category also largely influenced by federal programs.[7]

It is unlikely that the same reason applies to its effect on government administration spending. This positive relationship could indicate that the overall reduction in total expenditures induced by this practice conceals a redistribution of funds across budget categories. Some programs included in this category might benefit from this redistribution. For example,

[6]For an excellent overview of some of these rules, see Ransdell and Boloorian (2002, 2005).

[7]Unfortunately, the NASBO surveys provide no indication of the form that funding targets take.

reductions in spending in other areas could be channeled toward tax relief or some types of general-purpose assistance to local governments.

Legislative Access

Likewise, most expenditure categories are reduced when legislative access is implemented. The effect is statistically significant for government administration, environment and housing, higher education, social services, and transportation spending (Figure 4.6). Legislative access increases health expenditures by 1.8 percent. Although the effect cannot be rejected as being statistically different from 0, it is consistent with a scenario in which the additional information contained in budget requests allows legislators to oversee potentially excessive spending plans in some areas (e.g., government administration) while they simultaneously redistribute expenditures toward other categories (in this case, health services). In this particular case, the increase in health expenditures is not large enough to

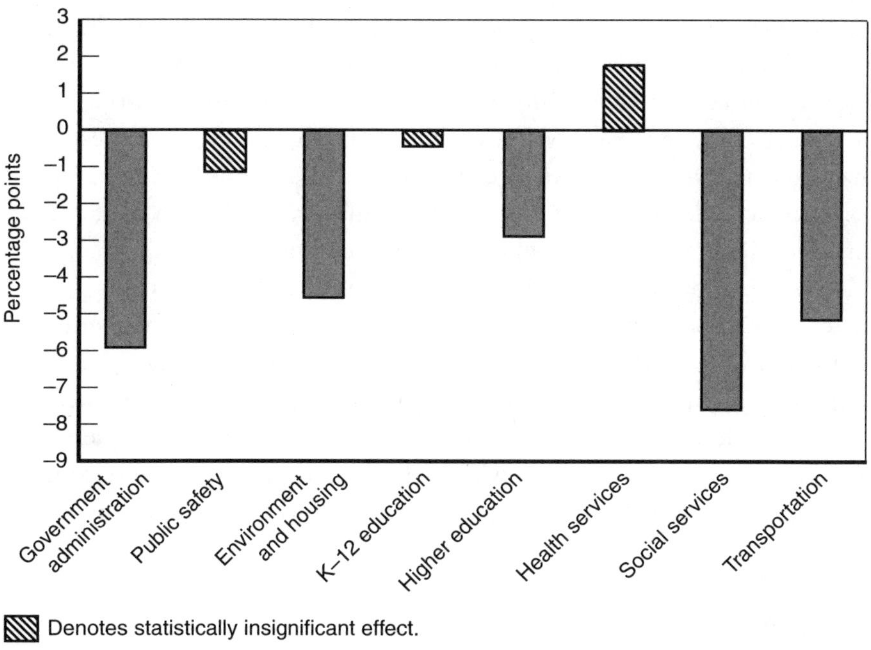

Figure 4.6—The Effect of Legislative Access on State Expenditures, by Spending Category

increase total expenditures alone, but the higher spending in this category is partially financed through the reallocation of funds that would go to one or several other categories.

Performance Budgeting

To analyze the effects of performance budgeting on individual categories, it was necessary to distinguish the cases where states followed this practice by specific area. Recall that in the case of total expenditures, a state is classified as using performance budgeting (or any other performance-related practice) if the practice is applied to at least one government area. For example, states that use performance budgeting only for environment and housing will be classified as having the practice, so will those states that use performance budgeting for all government areas.

Using these classifications, the results show that performance budgeting induces a statistically significant reduction in expenditures in K–12 education. Statistically insignificant reductions are also seen in public safety, health services, social services, and higher education (Figure 4.7). This result is consistent with the hypothesis that performance budgeting is conducive to eliminating unnecessary spending and thus to increasing efficiency. However, it is also consistent with the hypothesis that programs in this area are receiving smaller allocations because their performance is below expectations. Unfortunately, the data do not allow distinguishing between these alternative explanations.

Spending for the environment and housing and transportation increases with performance budgeting. One reason may be that a better knowledge of the outcomes in these two areas because of this practice might make budget participants and taxpayers more reluctant to reduce expenditure levels or more willing to support larger budgets. Another could be that this increased knowledge provides arguments for additional funding, through boosting performance with additional resources or rewarding the good results of some programs.

Summary

The statistical evidence suggests that changing the budgeting process through adoption or elimination of some practices can lead to changes

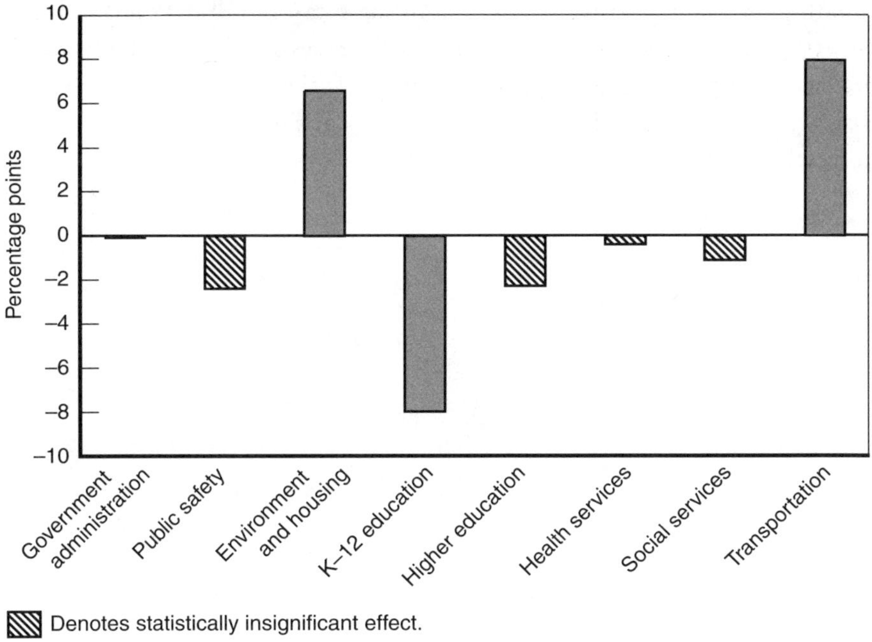

Figure 4.7—The Effect of Performance Budgeting on State Expenditures, by Spending Category

in expenditure levels: Three of the six budget practices characterized as relevant for expenditures reduce expenditures in a statistically significant way. The channels through which this happens differ, but the results for the practice of legislative access are consistent with the theory that increased information among budget participants and throughout the process plays an important role. Specific policy instructions (funding targets) and practices related to increased rationality of funding decisions (performance budgeting) also contribute to leaner budgets. The reductions or increases in total state government expenditures associated with each practice are relatively moderate, representing less than 3 percent of total spending. Also, there is evidence suggesting that the strength of these effects differs according to the number of years each practice has been in effect.

Finally, there is evidence that different practices affect government spending categories in different ways. Although the effects are generally in line with their relationship to overall expenditures, they differ in magnitude (funding targets, legislative access) and in some cases in direction (funding targets, performance budgeting). These differences suggest that budget practices affect the budget process's funding decisions through more than one mechanism, raising some important considerations for their implementation.

5. Benefits and Challenges of California's Budget Process Reform

This report has described the budget practices likely to have an effect on state expenditures, has identified which have been adopted in California and in other states, and has discussed their effects on government spending. This concluding chapter offers an outline of which changes are available to California now and their consequences for expenditures. It also offers some thoughts on whether the monetary benefits of such reforms are likely to outweigh their nonmonetary costs and to overcome possible obstacles for their implementation.

It is important to remember that the interest in exploring modifications to budget practices stems largely from repeated calls for budget process reform. This phenomenon is neither exclusive to California nor a new one in the state (Wear Simmons, 2002). Interest in the budget process tends to arise in economically adverse times. Because of the nature of economic cycles, it is likely that California will face dire fiscal circumstances again in the future, and that those in policy and academic circles will issue new calls for reviewing the budget process.

The effectiveness of budget practices can be measured along several dimensions, such as the ability to construct a budget on time, the budget's transparency, accountability, revenues, or expenditures. The report has focused on this last dimension for two reasons—because it is an easily comprehensible budgetary outcome that affects the public directly and because claims that some practices help reduce government spending have not received systematic examination.

Possibilities for Reform

California's budget process already incorporates some of the budget practices studied in this report. Since its early years, California has followed a budget process in which the executive branch dictates most of the budget agenda. Inherently, such a process allows for the possibility that the executive branch will instruct government agencies to adhere to specific funding targets in their initial budget requests. In fact, the Department of Finance has instructed government agencies to adhere to funding targets in the past. Similarly, California's May revision tradition has allowed updating of revenue and caseload forecast figures during the legislative session for some time.

The results in Chapter 4 suggest that funding targets have reduced expenditures whenever they have been used but not that California's May revision has also done so. The first result suggests that California could change the nature of funding targets, adopting them as a permanent practice instead of their current sporadic and discretionary use, and the second provides insufficient justification for abandoning the May revision. The two options left for California are permitting legislative access to budget requests during the first stage of the budget process and implementing a performance budgeting system.

The results from the multivariate analysis in Chapter 4 indicate that states that allow legislative access reduced their spending by 2.1 percent on average. The resulting expenditure reductions were concentrated on government administration, environment and housing, higher education, social services, and transportation. A back-of-the-envelope calculation—keeping in mind that this estimate reflects how long this practice has been in effect in other states—suggests that the reduction in expenditures associated with legislative access would be equivalent to an annual average reduction in California's state budget of $188 million. At the same time, it is important to underscore that these reductions in spending levels would not necessarily be achieved immediately after adopting this practice and that there is evidence that the attained reductions fade with time.

California could also enact reforms to allocate funds based on agencies' performance. States with a budgeting system based on performance indicators spend 2 percent less than states exclusively following the more traditional incremental budgeting. Taking into account the average number of years this practice had been in place in the period of analysis in other states, this would represent an average annual reduction in California's total spending of $1.2 billion. However, policymakers should not expect to see these reductions consistently year by year. The empirical evidence suggests that these reductions are not evenly distributed across time, with performance budgeting having only moderate effects immediately after its implementation and after more than ten years of being in effect. Spending on K–12 education is the area with the most significant reductions in expenditures associated with performance budgeting.

Challenges of Reform

The question of whether California should embrace changes in its budget process, and, if so, which ones, does not have straightforward answers. If the sole goal of reforming the budget process was to keep government spending in check, only extremely low nonpecuniary implementation costs (e.g., strong political will to make those reforms or minimal opposition to fragmenting budgetary powers) would make such changes a worthy exercise. An assessment of such costs requires information not readily available and is beyond the scope of this study. Nevertheless, it is useful to outline which reforms are likely to pay for themselves.

California has in the past used funding targets that instruct government agencies to limit their budget requests by specific amounts. This practice has reduced expenditures across the states using it during the years of this study, 1988–2000. The only consideration for the executive branch is whether to incorporate funding targets explicitly as a permanent requirement to develop budget requests. This change would not necessarily require a substantial reform in California and would likely face little or no political resistance.

Enabling legislative access to budget requests before preparation of the governor's budget might be more complicated. Adopting this practice is likely to be relatively easy from the administration's point of view, since government agencies already prepare budget requests and disclose them to the Department of Finance. However, political costs are likely to play a pivotal role. The confidentiality of budget requests stems from the need to keep executive unity and control of the budget—one of the main concerns when California's modern budgeting system was designed in the early 20th century. The yearly budget letters at the beginning of the budget cycle explicitly remind agencies of the requests' confidential nature. It is not clear whether the change in balance of budgetary power generated by this practice enjoys consensus among policymakers.

A last possibility for reforming the budgeting process in California is the adoption of a performance-based budgeting system. However, it is important to remember that California's previous attempt to adopt performance budgeting was short-lived (see Chapter 3). Among the many reasons for not renewing the state's pilot programs was the perception that a performance budgeting system was not conducive to reducing expenditures. The results presented in this report show that there are indeed fiscal benefits to following a performance-based budgeting system but also that they could be infrequent and in cases take several years to materialize.

It is of course not possible to tell if California would have witnessed substantial spending reductions had it chosen to maintain its performance budgeting pilots. The scope of those agencies' implementation of the trial programs was limited and did not represent a significant share of the state budget. At the same time, other states such as Florida and Oregon started their current performance-based management and budgeting systems with pilot programs that resembled California's pilots but later expanded them to all government agencies. It then seems as though the duration, rather than the magnitude, of performance budgeting's costs and benefits might play the most significant role in sustaining the change in the way funds are allocated among agencies and programs under this system.

Performance budgeting has the strongest negative association with K–12 education expenditures. This area enjoys strong support among Californians, who would rather see their funding levels go up, not down (Baldassare, 2007). More important, the presence of the constitutional spending guarantee of Proposition 98 could severely hinder the expense-cutting capacity of this practice. Further, these are all political, not fiscal, costs that must be considered.

In sum, California does have some options if it wishes to introduce to its budget process new practices that have the potential to cut spending. The prospects for those reforms' implementation, however, are in doubt given their relatively high political costs. The moderate spending reductions associated with alternative budget practices suggest that if substantial cost controls are the paramount goal, California should explore other possibilities, focusing reform on reinforcing the rules and practices (such as balanced budget rules, expenditure limits, or supermajority requirements for tax increases) already in place to make them more effective budgetary tools.

But the budget practices studied in this report could also bring benefits beyond reduced expenditures, such as more transparent and efficient provision of government services and increased accountability. Indirect benefits of improved management of fiscal affairs might include an enhanced perception of the state's creditworthiness and an increased disposition among the state's taxpayers to support other fiscal reforms. Finally, some budget practices tilt the power to make budgetary decisions away from the executive and place more importance in the legislature, and these are likely to have important political implications. Evaluating the effect of budget practices on all these outcomes presents different challenges, but it certainly merits further investigation.

Appendix A
Data Sources

Information on budget practices for the 50 states used in this report came from several sources. The first is the series of reports entitled *Budget Processes in the States*, published by NASBO. Started in 1976, these surveys provide information on a plethora of procedures and characteristics of the budget functions, powers, and practices, mostly of the executive branch. Examples include budget timelines and participants, gubernatorial budgetary authority, requirements and limitations, budget practices, and budget contents and post-enactment monitoring. These reports are based on a survey sent to the budget offices in each state and are the main source for data on the use of funding targets as a guideline for budget requests and on the availability of budget revisions within the period of legislative discussion of the budget plan. The surveys were published in 1977, 1981, 1987, 1989, 1992, 1995, 1997, 1999, and 2002.

Legislative Budget Procedures, a series of surveys focused on legislative appropriations procedures and published by the National Conference of State Legislatures (NCSL), is the second main source of data. The information in these surveys encompasses the legislative budget calendar, characteristics of the budget bill, procedures to develop and deliberate over the budget, as well as post-enactment revisions and requirements. Some of its questions overlap those in the NASBO surveys (such as the existence of line-item veto authority and supermajority requirements for tax increases) but there is no overlap for the information on budget practices. These surveys provide information on legislative access to budget requests before receipt of the budget plan. The NCSL published these reports in 1976, 1988, and 1998.

Even though these publications have existed since at least 1976, the availability and level of information differ from year to year. In particular, data on mid-session revisions were unavailable before 1988. In addition, since NASBO started to collect information on performance-related practices only in its 1995 survey, it was necessary to match the year at which states implemented performance-related practices from surveys by

Melkers and Willoughby (1998), and Crain and O'Roark (2004), as well as from budget offices' websites for the states for which these authors did not have information. These states are Alaska, Hawaii, Indiana, Maryland, Massachusetts, New Mexico, Tennessee, and Wyoming.

The report classifies a state as following performance measurement if it does so in all government areas or at least in one of them. Performance management and budgeting follow the same definition, except that they are conditioned on the state reporting that it practices performance measurement, because in some cases, states report that they follow performance management or budgeting but not that they develop performance measures, which are necessary for the other two practices. Finally, a state is considered to follow performance-related practices in a particular government area if it follows them either in all government categories or in the government area of interest.

The data sources described above provide a categorical characterization of budget practices; that is, they indicate whether at a given time each state followed a specific practice. Thus, each practice is measured as a dichotomous variable taking the value of 1 whenever a practice is in place and 0 otherwise. This is not without problems. In particular, the surveys do not provide information on the level of discretion or legal nature of some practices. More important, the dichotomous nature of the information does not provide any further detail on how a particular practice is implemented. For example, it is not possible to tell whether funding targets are expressed in dollars or as a percentage of some previous value or if performance measures refer to outcomes of specific programs or outputs at the overall-agency level. In addition, the time interval between surveys is never shorter than two years, which prevents pinning down the exact year in which a practice is adopted or abandoned. Nevertheless, the state and time coverage is quite good, and since these data sources provide unique measures of each practice, they enable the first-ever characterization of the use across the nation of budget practices with potential fiscal implications.

The U.S. Bureau of the Census's publication *Government Finance Statistics* provided information on total government expenditures and by spending category. The Census Bureau was also the source for demographic information, mainly through its *Current Population Survey*.

Citizen and government ideology indices were developed by Berry et al. (1998) and extracted from the corresponding unpublished supplement.

The definitions of government areas by NASBO and of spending categories by the Census of Governments are somewhat different. To conduct the analysis of the effect of performance-related practices on spending categories, the report matches the NASBO and Bureau of Census definitions, respectively, in the following way: natural resources, environment, and economic development with environment and housing; health and human services with both health services and social services; public safety with public safety; transportation with transportation; education with both K–12 and higher education; and administration with government administration (equal to the sum of general government and other government). Table A.1 presents the summary statistics of the variables used in this study.

Table A.1

The Key Characteristics of States, 1988–2000

	Mean	Standard Deviation
State government expenditures	3,170	1,069
Personal income	26,497	4,168
Transfers from the federal government	1,755	575
% population age < 18	25.97	2.19
% population age > 64	12.47	2.02
% population nonwhite	16.78	12.20
% population in metropolitan areas	65.22	21.19
Unemployment rate	5.23	1.54
Citizen ideology index	48.52	14.40
Government ideology index	49.24	24.80
Tax/expenditure limits (= 1 if yes)	0.47	0.49
Line-item veto (= 1 if yes)	0.81	0.39
Supermajority required for tax increases (= 1 if yes)	0.22	0.41
Funding targets (= 1 if yes)	0.53	0.50
Legislative access (= 1 if yes)	0.77	0.42
Performance measurement in at least one government area (= 1 if yes)	0.44	0.50
Performance management in at least one government area (= 1 if yes)	0.33	0.47
Performance budgeting in at least one government area (= 1 if yes)	0.34	0.47
Mid-session revision (= 1 if yes)	0.46	0.50

NOTE: Monetary variables are in 2002 per capita dollars.

Appendix B
Methods and Regression Results

This report uses data on a panel of the 50 U.S. states from 1988 to 2000 to estimate the following extension of the standard public goods expenditure model:

$$E_{it} = \beta Z_{it} + \gamma X_{it} + u_i + \lambda_t + \varepsilon_{it} \ . \qquad \text{(B.1)}$$

In Eq. (B.1), the effect of budget practices on government spending in state *i* at time *t* (E_{it}) is identified by a set of indicator variables Z_{it} taking the value of 1 when a state follows a particular practice and 0 otherwise. To account for other socioeconomic conditions affecting government spending policies across states, the set of controls X_{it} includes personal income, intergovernmental grants from the federal government, demographic composition of the population (percentage under age 18, above age 64, and nonwhite), the unemployment rate, the percentage of the population living in metropolitan areas, indexes of citizen and government ideology, an indicator variable for governments in which the governor's party is different from the party with control of the state's legislature, and indicator variables for the presence of tax and expenditure limits, gubernatorial line-item veto power, and supermajority requirements for tax increases. State (u_i) and year (λ_t) fixed effects control for time- and state-invariant unobservable characteristics, respectively.

In addition, it is necessary to account for the possibility that budget practices are endogenous. This could occur for two reasons. First, states that have particular preferences for spending levels—for example, because of political culture or attitudes toward the size of government—might be more likely to adopt (or not) certain practices. Second, the adoption of a practice in a given state might be prompted by the economic circumstances at a particular time. Thus, ordinary least squares (OLS) fixed-effect estimates from Eq. (B.1) provide evidence of correlation between a particular budget practice and state expenditures but say nothing about the spending consequences of adopting a practice. To correctly address this problem, the report uses an instrumental variable (IV) approach by adding an equation for each budget practice of the form:

$$Z_{kit} = \delta_1 X_{it} + \delta_2 W_{kit} + \varphi_i + \theta_t + \nu_{kit} . \tag{B.2}$$

In Eq. (B.2), Z_{kit} is practice *k* in state *i* at time *t*, the variables X_{it} are defined as before, and W_{kit} is a set of variables that satisfy two conditions for each practice *k*: (1) They must be correlated with the propensity of state *i* to adopt practice *k* but (2) must not determine expenditures directly.[1] Also, φ_i and θ_t are state and time fixed effects defined analogously as those in Eq. (B.1). For this study, I estimate the propensity of a state to have each practice in a given year as a function of the number of states implementing that same practice in the rest of the country (i.e., excluding that particular state) the previous year and two years before. These instruments are motivated by the fact that many states conduct or refer to case studies on previous experiences with budget practices before deciding whether to adopt them. Thus, the number of states using a particular practice will correlate with its use in other states through this evaluation process. Furthermore, a particular state's spending is unlikely to be influenced by budget practices elsewhere, and so the proposed variables will satisfy the two conditions for being valid instruments.

To estimate the relationship between total expenditures and each budget practice through time, I created an indicator variable for each year a particular practice had been in effect during the sample period. That is, the variable for "one year in effect" was set equal to 1 if the practice was in its first year—regardless of the calendar year of adoption—and 0 in all other years, including those in which the practice was in effect beyond the first year. The indicator variable for "two years in effect" was equal to 1 in the second year a particular state followed a practice and equal to 0 all other years it was in effect, including the first (implementation) year. Variables for longer periods of "time in effect" were defined analogously.

The information on the use of all budget practices was available for years after 1977, with the exception of information on mid-session revisions, which was available only in 1988 and subsequent years.

---

[1] This second condition is equivalent to requiring that ε_{it} and ν_{kit} be uncorrelated.

Therefore, it is possible that at the beginning of the period of analysis (1988), states had already followed some practices for several years. In addition, some practices were already in effect in 1977 but it is impossible to know how long states had followed them at that point in time. This creates a classification dilemma. On the one hand, assigning these cases the indicator variable "one year in effect" would bias the estimates for this variable when it is measured correctly. The solution is to put those cases in a separate category labeled "in effect since at least 1977 (1988 for mid-session revisions)" and not decompose them by year in effect. On the other hand, this correction imposes a different bias in the coefficients of practices by year in effect because it excludes observations corresponding to some years.

The first type of bias is likely to increase with the number of states that already followed that practice at that time but is likely to be small the fewer the states that fall into this category. For the sample period, 51 percent of observations followed legislative access since at least 1977 and 36 percent followed mid-session revisions since at least 1988. Thus, I made the correction of creating a separate "in effect since at least . . ." category for these two variables.[2] In turn, the number of observations that followed the remaining budget practices since at least 1977 was small (6% for funding targets and slightly over 5% for the performance trio), and as a consequence I did not distinguish them from the first and subsequent years in effect.

Instrumental variables regressions were impractical for estimating how expenditures were affected by budget practices through time because of the high number of potentially endogenous variables that result from decomposing the effect of each practice by number of years in effect. Hence, the report presents results from standard OLS within (fixed-effects) estimation in these cases. Although this means that the resulting coefficients should not be interpreted as causal effects, OLS and IV estimates are very similar (see Table B.1). Thus, these coefficients are a reasonably good approximation of the time it takes for each budget practice

[2]These variables will then reflect standard within (fixed-effects) estimators for those cases and should be interpreted as average relationships over the short and long terms.

Table B.1

The Determinants of State per Capita Expenditures

	IV Estimates	OLS Estimates
Funding targets (= 1 if yes)	−0.017*	−0.013*
	(0.008)	(0.006)
Legislative access (= 1 if yes)	−0.021*	−0.021**
	(0.010)	(0.008)
Performance measurement in at least one government area (= 1 if yes)	0.019	0.021*
	(0.013)	(0.009)
Performance management in at least one government area (= 1 if yes)	−0.005	−0.006
	(0.012)	(0.007)
Performance budgeting in at least one government area (= 1 if yes)	−0.020+	−0.024**
	(0.012)	(0.008)
Mid-session revision (= 1 if yes)	−0.018	−0.009
	(0.012)	(0.008)
Personal income	0.666**	0.533**
	(0.139)	(0.136)
Federal intergovernmental grants	0.344**	0.346**
	(0.035)	(0.027)
% of population age < 18	−0.012*	−0.015**
	(0.005)	(0.004)
% of population age > 64	−0.034**	−0.047**
	(0.012)	(0.012)
% of population nonwhite	−0.002+	0.0001
	(0.001)	(0.0004)
% of population in metropolitan areas	0.004**	0.001
	(0.002)	(0.001)
Unemployment rate	0.002	0.005+
	(0.004)	(0.003)
Citizen ideology index	−0.0002	−0.0001
	(0.001)	(0.0004)
Government ideology index	0.0001	0.0003+
	(0.0001)	(0.0001)
Divided government (= 1 if yes)	0.002	0.007
	(0.005)	(0.005)
Tax/expenditure limits (= 1 if yes)	−0.006	−0.013
	(0.011)	(0.008)
Line-item veto (= 1 if yes)	0.0001	0.011
	(0.001)	(0.009)
Supermajority required for tax increases (= 1 if yes)	0.011	0.003
	(0.012)	(0.010)

Table B.1 (continued)

	IV Estimates	OLS Estimates
No. of observations	550	650
R-squared	0.82	0.86

NOTES: Robust standard errors clustered by state are in parentheses.
+Denotes statistically significant difference at the 10 percent level.
*Denotes statistically significant difference at the 5 percent level.
**Denotes statistically significant difference at the 1 percent level.

to affect expenditures but not of the magnitude of the effects at each point in time.

The effects of budget practices on spending categories were estimated separately by category (equation by equation) using the same method as with total expenditures. All spending category equations control for real per capita income, citizen and government ideology indexes, indicators of divided government, tax and expenditure limits, supermajority requirements for tax increases, gubernatorial line-item veto, and state and year fixed effects. However, the specification of each equation differs by category-specific controls (listed in Table B.5, below).

All regressions use the natural logarithm of monetary variables, including state expenditures, to improve the fit of the models. Thus, the estimated coefficient of each budget practice is transformed to calculate the percentage change in expenditures associated with it in the following way (Kennedy, 1981):

$$\Delta = e^{\hat{\beta} - \hat{\sigma}_{\beta}^{2}/2} - 1 \,. \qquad \text{(B.3)}$$

In Eq. (B.3), e is Euler's number, Δ is the percentage change in expenditures, $\hat{\beta}$ is the estimated coefficient of any given budget practice, and $\hat{\sigma}_{\beta}$ its associated standard error. The tables that follow report the estimated coefficients $\hat{\beta}$, and the report's main text refers to the transformed percentage changes Δ.

Table B.1 presents the estimates of the relationship of budget practices with total expenditures. This table also presents the estimated coefficients of all socioeconomic controls. For completeness and comparison, the fixed-effects estimates obtained from OLS are included in the second column of this table. For brevity, the estimated coefficients of the corresponding socioeconomic controls are not included in subsequent tables.

The "first stage" estimates for the budget practice equations are in Table B.2. In general, they indicate that after controlling for socioeconomic and political factors, states are less likely to adopt a particular budget practice if more states had it in place the year before they decide to adopt it but more likely to incorporate it into their budget process if more states have it in place two years before the date adoption. An interpretation of these results is that states evaluate not only which states or how many states had a practice in the immediate past (the first lag) but also concentrate on practices that have survived for more than one period (the second lag). This might suggest that states are very cautious about adopting a budget practice even when other states have it in place. Finally, the adoption of a particular budget practice is generally not influenced by the presence of other budget practices in other states (e.g., adopting *funding targets* in California is independent of the number of states besides California that used *mid-session revisions* in the past). This result suggests that states do not typically focus on the adoption of several practices at the time or that they incorporate potential interactions between practices in their decisions on whether to adopt a practice. Table B.3 displays a set of specification tests for the validity of the instruments and confirms that they are appropriate.

Table B.4 presents the estimates for the relationship between state expenditures and each budget practice by years in effect since 1977. Legislative access was not significantly correlated with expenditures when it was in place since at least 1977, suggesting that its effects on expenditures dissipate beyond their 19th year in place. By contrast, mid-session revisions had no significant correlation with spending during the first seven years in effect, but their relationship with expenditures was statistically significant if the practice was in place since at least 1988. This result suggests that if mid-session revisions have any effects on spending, they materialize mostly in the long term.

Finally, Table B.5 lists the control variables (in addition to budget practices) specific to each spending category. Table B.6 contains the IV estimates of the effects of budget practices for the corresponding equations.

Table B.2

The Determinants of the Adoption of Budget Practices

	Funding Targets	Legislative Access	Performance Measurement	Performance Management	Performance Budgeting	Mid-Session Revision
Personal income	–0.051	–0.789*	0.662	0.391	0.815	0.161
	(0.442)	(0.360)	(0.754)	(0.751)	(0.766)	(0.287)
Federal intergovernmental grants	–0.038	0.154+	–0.717**	–0.769**	–0.841**	–0.083
	(0.128)	(0.079)	(0.242)	(0.218)	(0.217)	(0.095)
% of population age < 18	–0.033*	–0.012	–0.057*	–0.060*	–0.055*	0.014
	(0.016)	(0.012)	(0.028)	(0.026)	(0.028)	(0.014)
% of population age > 64	–0.002	–0.067*	0.111+	0.032	0.081	0.017
	(0.030)	(0.030)	(0.058)	(0.052)	(0.059)	(0.018)
% of population nonwhite	0.001	0.003*	0.001	0.004	0.005	0.000
	(0.002)	(0.001)	(0.004)	(0.004)	(0.004)	(0.001)
% of population in metropolitan areas	0.010+	–0.006	0.008	0.011	0.009	0.000
	(0.006)	(0.004)	(0.008)	(0.008)	(0.008)	(0.004)
Unemployment rate	0.017	0.010	–0.044+	–0.015	0.019	0.007
	(0.013)	(0.010)	(0.025)	(0.023)	(0.024)	(0.008)
Citizen ideology index	–0.002	–0.003+	0.008**	0.010**	0.007**	0.000
	(0.002)	(0.002)	(0.003)	(0.003)	(0.003)	(0.002)
Government ideology index	0.000	0.000	–0.001	–0.002*	–0.001	0.000
	(0.001)	(0.001)	(0.001)	(0.001)	(0.001)	—
Divided government (= 1 if yes)	0.008	–0.005	0.003	–0.005	0.011	–0.020
	(0.019)	(0.014)	(0.035)	(0.031)	(0.038)	(0.019)

Table B.2 (continued)

	Funding Targets	Legislative Access	Performance Measurement	Performance Management	Performance Budgeting	Mid-Session Revision
Tax/expenditure limits (= 1 if yes)	−0.083	0.032	0.197**	0.220**	0.234**	0.026
	(0.052)	(0.037)	(0.071)	(0.067)	(0.071)	(0.036)
Line-item veto (= 1 if yes)	0.037	−0.040	0.064	−0.002	0.044	0.073
	(0.050)	(0.041)	(0.082)	(0.075)	(0.081)	(0.050)
Supermajority required for tax increases (= 1 if yes)	0.008	0.003	0.017	0.088	0.062	−0.043**
	(0.032)	(0.025)	(0.075)	(0.061)	(0.076)	(0.016)
No. of states with funding targets the previous year	−0.801**	−0.029	−0.014	−0.034	−0.079	−0.005
	(0.043)	(0.050)	(0.073)	(0.071)	(0.061)	(0.020)
No. of states with funding targets two years before	0.068*	0.131*	0.078	0.177*	0.143*	0.032+
	(0.028)	(0.059)	(0.081)	(0.080)	(0.071)	(0.017)
No. of states with legislative access the prevous year	0.040	−0.830**	−0.016	0.041	0.070	0.086
	(0.062)	(0.039)	(0.084)	(0.076)	(0.094)	(0.060)
No. of states with legislative access two years before	−0.005	0.010	0.027	0.012	−0.035	−0.062
	(0.057)	(0.014)	(0.084)	(0.073)	(0.090)	(0.055)
No. of states with performance measurement the previous year	0.047	0.042	−0.681**	0.030	0.030	−0.011
	(0.042)	(0.073)	(0.062)	(0.058)	(0.065)	(0.035)
No. of states with performance measurement two years before	−0.029	−0.023	0.385**	0.174**	0.193**	0.049+
	(0.040)	(0.079)	(0.065)	(0.058)	(0.061)	(0.029)

Table B.2 (continued)

	Funding Targets	Legislative Access	Performance Measurement	Performance Management	Performance Budgeting	Mid-Session Revision
No. of states with performance	–0.052	0.031	0.058	–0.671**	0.045	–0.009
management the previous year	(0.034)	(0.056)	(0.059)	(0.072)	(0.063)	(0.028)
No. of states with performance	–0.012	–0.045	–0.151*	0.097	–0.082	0.021
management two years before	(0.034)	(0.066)	(0.064)	(0.073)	(0.069)	(0.026)
No. of states with performance	–0.054	–0.076	–0.025	–0.052	–0.722**	0.029
budgeting the previous year	(0.037)	(0.068)	(0.055)	(0.059)	(0.069)	(0.046)
No. of states with performance	0.053	0.072	–0.073	–0.094	0.088	–0.068+
budeting two years before	(0.039)	(0.076)	(0.060)	(0.065)	(0.058)	(0.035)
No. of states with mid-session revisions	0.005	0.048	0.011	0.025	–0.004	–0.811**
the prevous year	(0.040)	(0.070)	(0.067)	(0.074)	(0.063)	(0.051)
No. of states with mid-session revisions	0.041	0.000	–0.093	–0.129	–0.110+	0.023
two years before	(0.038)	(0.076)	(0.064)	(0.081)	(0.059)	(0.022)
No. of observations	550	550	550	550	550	550
R-squared	0.65	0.74	0.56	0.56	0.49	0.70

NOTES: Robust standard errors clustered by state are in parentheses.
+Denotes statistically significant at the 10 percent level.
*Denotes statistically significant at the 5 percent level.
**Denotes statistically significant at the 1 percent level.

Table B.3

Specification Tests for the Instrumental Variables Model

Overidentification test (Ho: model is not overidentified)	
Chi-squared stat (d.f. = 6)	5.12
p-value	0.53
Redundancy of instruments test; first lag (Ho: instruments are redundant)	
Chi-squared stat (d.f. = 36)	1,404
p-value	0.00
Redundancy of instruments test; second lag (Ho: instruments are redundant)	
Chi-squared stat (d.f. = 36)	96.50
p-value	0.00
Joint significance of instruments in reduced form equation	
F (12, 49) statistic	1.10
p-value	0.38

Table B.4

The Relationship Between Total Expenditures and Budget Practices, by Years in Effect, 1988–2000

Years in Effect	Funding Targets	Legislative Access	Performance Measurement	Performance Management	Performance Budgeting	Mid-Session Revision
1	–0.001	–0.037	**0.022***	–0.010	**–0.031***	0.001
	(0.009)	(0.026)	**(0.010)**	(0.009)	**(0.008)**	(0.013)
2	–0.011	**–0.039***	**0.025***	–0.005	**–0.023***	–0.024
	(0.010)	**(0.017)**	**(0.011)**	(0.010)	**(0.010)**	(0.018)
3	**–0.020***	**–0.044***	**0.029***	–0.006	**–0.030****	–0.002
	(0.009)	**(0.018)**	**(0.012)**	(0.010)	**(0.010)**	(0.012)
4	**–0.017+**	**–0.051****	**0.035****	0.005	**–0.020+**	–0.008
	(0.009)	**(0.016)**	**(0.012)**	(0.011)	**(0.012)**	(0.018)
5	–0.011	**–0.049+**	**0.040****	0.001	–0.016	0.007
	(0.010)	**(0.027)**	**(0.015)**	(0.013)	(0.016)	(0.031)
6	**–0.023***	**–0.084****	**0.023+**	–0.004	–0.015	0.010
	(0.010)	**(0.025)**	**(0.012)**	(0.018)	(0.019)	(0.018)
7	–0.008	**–0.048****	**0.030***	–0.004	–0.010	0.005
	(0.013)	**(0.017)**	**(0.014)**	(0.024)	(0.022)	(0.016)
8	–0.015	**–0.039****	**0.026***	–0.007	–0.026	
	(0.015)	**(0.014)**	**(0.012)**	(0.014)	(0.018)	
9	0.008	**–0.031+**	**0.020+**	–0.014	**–0.034+**	
	(0.015)	**(0.017)**	**(0.012)**	(0.015)	**(0.020)**	

Table B.4 (continued)

Years in Effect	Funding Targets	Legislative Access	Performance Measurement	Performance Management	Performance Budgeting	Mid-Session Revision
10	0.024	−0.019	**0.025***	−0.014	−0.011	
	(0.015)	(0.016)	**(0.015)**	(0.019)	(0.016)	
11	0.004	**−0.069****	**0.022+**	−0.009	−0.017	
	(0.014)	**(0.021)**	**(0.011)**	(0.013)	(0.016)	
12	−0.005	**−0.057****	−0.021	**−0.055+**	**−0.079+**	
	(0.016)	**(0.020)**	(0.033)	**(0.033)**	**(0.042)**	
13	−0.001	**−0.035***	−0.027	**−0.060***	**−0.082****	
	(0.016)	**(0.017)**	(0.029)	**(0.028)**	**(0.029)**	
14	−0.012	**−0.031+**	−0.018	**−0.051***	**−0.072****	
	(0.018)	**(0.017)**	(0.024)	**(0.022)**	**(0.024)**	
15	−0.011	−0.022	−0.006	−0.039	**−0.060***	
	(0.022)	(0.015)	(0.026)	(0.024)	(0.025)	
16	**−0.068***	−0.021	0.043	0.011	−0.012	
	(0.029)	(0.016)	(0.031)	(0.029)	(0.031)	
17	**−0.072****	−0.025	0.015	−0.018	−0.039	
	(0.019)	(0.016)	(0.024)	(0.022)	(0.025)	
18	**−0.052***	**−0.030+**	0.023	−0.009	−0.030	
	(0.020)	**(0.018)**	(0.021)	(0.016)	(0.021)	

Table B.4 (continued)

Years in Effect	Funding Targets	Legislative Access	Performance Measurement	Performance Management	Performance Budgeting	Mid-Session Revision
19	**−0.049+**	**−0.051***	0.011	−0.021	**−0.043***	
	(0.025)	**(0.020)**	(0.022)	(0.017)	**(0.022)**	
20	−0.042		0.023		−0.033	
	(0.028)		(0.030)		(0.030)	
21	**−0.066***		0.033		−0.020	
	(0.028)		(0.029)		(0.030)	
22	**−0.057***					
	(0.024)					
23	−0.033					
	(0.021)					
24	0.004					
	(0.073)					
In place since		0.002				
at least 1977		(0.013)				
In place since						**−0.038***
at least 1988						**(0.019)**

NOTES: Robust standard errors clustered by state are in parentheses. Statistically significant coefficients are shown in boldface for ease of reading.

+Denotes statistically significant at the 10 percent level.

*Denotes statistically significant at the 5 percent level.

**Denotes statistically significant at the 1 percent level.

Table B.5

Category-Specific Control Variables

	Government Administration	Public Safety	Environment and Housing	K–12 Education	Higher Education	Health Services	Social Services	Transportation
Transfers from the federal government for								
General purpose	X	X	X	X	X	X	X	X
Environment and housing			X					
Education				X	X			
Health						X		
Social services							X	
Transportation								X
% of population age < 18						X	X	
% of population age > 64						X	X	
% of population nonwhite							X	
% of population in metropolitan areas		X	X					X

Table B.5 (continued)

	Government Administration	Public Safety	Environment and Housing	K–12 Education	Higher Education	Health Services	Social Services	Transportation
% of population enrolled in public schools				X				
% of population enrolled in degree-granting public institutions					X			
Unemployment rate		X					X	
% of population with income under federal poverty line						X	X	
Bottom quartile of income distribution						X	X	

Table B.6

The Effect of Budget Practices on State Expenditures, by Spending Category

	Government Administration	Public Safety	Environment and Housing	K–12 Education	Higher Education	Health Services	Social Services	Transportation
Funding targets	0.038+	−0.066**	−0.114**	−0.049**	−0.011	−0.013	0.056*	−0.038+
(= 1 if yes)	(0.020)	(0.021)	(0.022)	(0.017)	(0.014)	(0.021)	(0.027)	(0.021)
Legislative access	−0.060*	−0.011	−0.046+	−0.004	−0.029*	0.018	−0.078**	−0.052+
(= 1 if yes)	(0.030)	(0.024)	(0.024)	(0.028)	(0.012)	(0.020)	(0.027)	(0.027)
Performance measurement in at least one government area (= 1 if yes)	−0.014 (0.035)	(0.007) (0.029)	−0.081** (0.029)	0.102* (0.049)	0.007 (0.017)	−0.039 (0.032)	−0.025 (0.035)	−0.069 (0.043)
Performance management in at least one government area (= 1 if yes)	0.000 (0.038)	0.023 (0.028)	0.030 (0.032)	−0.065 (0.040)	−0.002 (0.016)	0.004 (0.027)	0.018 (0.036)	0.016 (0.037)
Performance budgeting in at least one government area (= 1 if yes)	0.000 (0.038)	−0.024 (0.028)	0.064* (0.030)	−0.082* (0.036)	−0.023 (0.016)	−0.004 (0.025)	−0.011 (0.033)	0.077+ (0.043)

Table B.6 (continued)

	Government Administration	Public Safety	Environment and Housing	K–12 Education	Higher Education	Health Services	Social Services	Transportation
Mid-session revision (= 1 if yes)	−0.061*	−0.139**	−0.003	0.047	−0.039**	−0.003	0.013	−0.063+
	(0.027)	(0.028)	(0.025)	(0.035)	(0.013)	(0.023)	(0.025)	(0.032)
No. of observations	550	550	550	550	550	550	550	550
R-squared	0.41	0.60	0.17	0.47	0.61	0.70	0.35	0.29

NOTE: Robust standard errors clustered by state are in parentheses.
+Denotes statistically significant difference at the 10 percent level.
*Denotes statistically significant difference at the 5 percent level.
**Denotes statistically significant difference at the 1 percent level.

Bibliography

Advisory Committee on Government Performance and Accountability, *Making Government Work for Oregonians: A Plan for Achieving Results-Based Government,* Oregon Progress Board, Salem, Oregon, January 2004.

Alt, James E., David Dreyer-Lassen, and David Skilling, "Fiscal Transparency, Gubernatorial Popularity, and the Scale of Government: Evidence from the States," mimeo, Harvard University and University of Copenhagen, 2001.

Bails, Dale, and Margie A. Tieslau, "The Impact of Fiscal Constitutions on State and Local Expenditure," *CATO Journal*, Vol. 20, No. 2, Fall 2000, pp. 255–277.

Baldassare, Mark, *PPIC Statewide Survey: Californians and Their Government*, Public Policy Institute of California, San Francisco, California, 2007.

Barrett, Katherine, Richard Greene, Zach Patton, and Michael Keeling, "Grading the States," *Governing*, February 2005.

Bergstrom, Theodore C., and Robert P. Goodman, "Private Demands for Public Goods," *American Economic Review*, Vol. 63, No. 3, June 1973, pp. 280–296.

Berry, William D., Evan J. Ringquist, Richard C. Fording, and Russell L. Hanson, "Measuring Citizen and Government Ideology in the American States, 1960–93," *American Journal of Political Science*, Vol. 42 , No. 1, January 1998, pp. 327–348.

Besley, Timothy, and Anne Case, "Political Institutions and Policy Choices: Evidence from the United States," *Journal of Economic Literature*, Vol. 41, No. 1, March 2003, pp. 7–73.

Brennan, Geoffrey, and James M. Buchanan, *The Power to Tax: Analytical Foundations of the Fiscal Constitution,* Cambridge University Press, Cambridge, Massachusetts, 1980.

Burns, Robert C., and Robert D. Lee, "The Ups and Downs of State Budget Process Reform: Experience of Three Decades," *Public Budgeting and Finance*, Vol. 24, No. 3, September 2004, pp. 1–19.

California Budget Project, *A Budget for All Californians: Improving the Transparency and Accountability of the State Budget,* Sacramento, California, May 2006.

California Department of Finance, *The Performance Budgeting Pilot Project: An Evaluation of Its Status,* Sacramento, California, January 1996.

California Legislative Analyst's Office, *Performance Budgeting: Will It Change the Budgeting Process?* Sacramento, California, February 1996.

California Performance Review, *The California Performance Review: Creating the First 21st Century Government in America,* Sacramento, California, 2004.

Council of State Governments, *The Book of the States*, Lexington, Kentucky, various years.

Crain, W. Mark, and Nicole V. Crain, "Fiscal Consequences of Budget Baselines," *Journal of Public Economics*, Vol. 67, No. 3, March 1998, pp. 421–436.

Crain, W. Mark, and J. Brian O'Roark, "The Impact of Performance-Based Budgeting on State Fiscal Performance," *Economics of Governance*, Vol. 5, No. 2, July 2004, pp. 167–186.

Ellwood, John W., and Mary Sprague, "Options for Reforming the California State Budget Process," in Bruce E. Cain and Roger G. Noll, eds., *Constitutional Reform in California: Making State Government More Effective,* Institute of Governmental Press, University of California, Berkeley, 1995.

Ferejohn, John, "Accountability and Authority: Toward a Theory of Political Accountability," in Adam Przeworski, Susan C. Stokes, and Bernard Manin, eds., *Democracy, Accountability and Representation*, Cambridge University Press, New York, 1999, pp. 131–153.

Fountain, Jay, *Case Study: State of Oregon. A Performance System Based on Benchmarks,* Governmental Accounting Standard Board, Norwalk, Connecticut, September 2002.

Goldstein, Morris, and Geoffrey Woglom, "Market-Based Fiscal Discipline in Monetary Unions: Evidence from the U.S. Municipal Bond Market," in M. B. Canzoneri, V. Grilli, and P. R. Masson, eds., *Establishing a Central Bank: Issues in Europe and Lessons from the U.S.*, Cambridge University Press, New York, 1992, pp. 228–270.

Holtz-Eakin, Douglas, "The Line Item Veto and Public Sector Budgets: Evidence from the States," *Journal of Public Economics*, Vol. 36, No. 3, August 1988, pp. 269–262.

Kennedy, Peter E., "Estimation with Correctly Interpreted Dummy Variables in Semilogarithmic Equations," *American Economic Review*, Vol. 71, No. 4, September 1981, p. 801.

Knight, Brian G., "Supermajority Voting Requirements for Tax Increases: Evidence from the States," *Journal of Public Economics*, Vol. 76, No. 1, April 2000, pp. 41–67.

Liner, Blaine, Pat Dusenbury, and Elisa Vinson, *State Approaches to Governing-for-Results and Accountability,* Urban Institute, Washington D.C., December 2000.

Little Hoover Commission, *Budget Reform: Putting Performance First,* Report No. 135, Sacramento, California, 1995.

Mackay, Robert J., and Carolyn L. Weaver, "Commodity Bundling and Agenda Control in the Public Sector," *Quarterly Journal of Economics*, Vol. 98, No. 4, November 1983, pp. 611–635.

Matsusaka, John G., "Economics of Direct Legislation," *Quarterly Journal of Economics*, Vol. 107, No. 2, May 1992, pp. 541–571.

Melkers, Julia, and Katherine Willoughby, "The State of the States: Performance-Based Budgeting Requirements in 47 out of 50," *Public Administration Review*, Vol. 58, No. 1, January/February 1998, pp. 66–73.

National Association of State Budget Officers, *Budgeting Processes in the States,* Washington, D.C., various years.

National Conference of State Legislatures, *Legislative Budget Procedures: A Guide to Appropriations and Budget Processes in the States Commonwealths and Territories,* Washington, D.C., various years.

National Conference of State Legislatures Fiscal Affairs, *Legislating for Results,* Washington, D.C., 2004.

Office of Program Policy Analysis and Government Accountability, *Performance-Based Program Budgeting in Context: History and Comparison,* Tallahassee, Florida, 1997.

Poterba, James M., "State Responses to Fiscal Crises: The Effects of Budgetary Institutions and Politics," *Journal of Political Economy*, Vol. 102, No. 4, August 1994a, pp. 799–821.

Poterba, James M., "Tax Policy Changes and the Pricing of Tax-Exempt Bonds," in Susan C. Heide, Robert A. Klein, and Hess Lederman, eds., *Handbook of Municipal Bonds,* Probus, Chicago, Illinois, 1994b.

Poterba, James M., "Do Budget Rules Work?" in Alan J. Auerbach, ed., *Fiscal Policy Lessons from Economic Research,* MIT Press, Cambridge, Massachusetts, 1997, pp. 53–86.

Poterba, James M., and Kim Rueben, "State Institutions and the U.S. Municipal Bond Market," in James M. Poterba and Jurgen von Hagen, eds., *Fiscal Institutions and Fiscal Performance,* Chicago University Press, Chicago, Illinois, 1999.

Ransdell, Tim, and Shervin Boloorian, *Federal Formula Grants: TANF and Welfare Programs,* Public Policy Institute of California, San Francisco, California, December 2002.

Ransdell, Tim, and Shervin Boloorian, *Federal Formula Grants: Federal Child Care Programs,* Public Policy Institute of California, San Francisco, California, June 2005.

Romer, Thomas, and Howard Rosenthal, "Bureaucrats Versus Voters: On the Political Economy of Resource Allocation by Direct Democracy," *Quarterly Journal of Economics*, Vol. 94, No. 4, November 1979, pp. 563–587.

Rueben, Kim, "Tax Limitations and Government Growth: The Effect of State Tax and Expenditure Limits on State and Local Government," mimeo, Public Policy Institute of California, San Francisco, California, 1997.

Shadbegian, Ronald J., "Do Tax and Expenditure Limitations Affect the Size and Growth of State Government?" *Contemporary Economic Policy*, Vol. 14, No. 1, January 1996, pp. 22–35.

Texas Senate Research Center, *Budget 101: A Guide to the Budget Process in Texas,* Austin, Texas, January 2005.

Wear Simmons, Charlene, "A Summary of Recommendations for Reforms to the State Budget Process," *California Research Bureau Note,* Vol. 9, No. 1, Sacramento, California, August 2002.

About the Author

JAIME CALLEJA ALDERETE

Jaime Calleja Alderete is a research fellow at the Public Policy Institute of California. His research interests include state and local public finance, intergovernmental fiscal relations, and political economy. He has written on the short- and long-term response of local expenditures to intergovernmental grants and his current research examines the role of budget rules and practices on state expenditures. He holds a B.A. in economics from the Instituto Tecnológico Autónomo de México and a Ph.D. in economics from Stanford University.

Related PPIC Publications

Fiscal Realities: Budget Tradeoffs in California Government (2007)
Tracy M. Gordon, Jaime Calleja Alderete, Patrick J. Murphy, Jon Sonstelie, Ping Zhang

Fiscal Effects of Voter Approval Requirements on Local Governments (2003)
Kim S. Rueben, Pedro Cerdán

Fiscal Rules and State Borrowing Costs: Evidence from California and Other States (1999)
James M. Poterba, Kim S. Rueben